GOD'S NAME IS
YAHWEH

TL Blaylock

WESTBOW
PRESS®
A DIVISION OF THOMAS NELSON
& ZONDERVAN

Scripture taken from the New King James Version®. Copyright ©
1982 by Thomas Nelson. Used by permission. All rights reserved.

WestBow Press books may be ordered through booksellers or by contacting:

WestBow Press
A Division of Thomas Nelson & Zondervan
1663 Liberty Drive
Bloomington, IN 47403
www.westbowpress.com
1 (866) 928-1240

Because of the dynamic nature of the Internet, any web addresses or
links contained in this book may have changed since publication and
may no longer be valid. The views expressed in this work are solely those
of the author and do not necessarily reflect the views of the publisher,
and the publisher hereby disclaims any responsibility for them.

Edited by Ryan Moore

ISBN: 978-1-5127-6090-3 (sc)
ISBN: 978-1-5127-6091-0 (hc)
ISBN: 978-1-5127-6089-7 (e)

Library of Congress Control Number: 2016917278

Print information available on the last page.

WestBow Press rev. date: 04/15/2020

CONTENTS

GOD IS LOVE

Love is as essential to life as the air we breathe. Just how far will we go to find love? Is love the reason we work like we do or play like we do? If I work long enough or hard enough will true love find a way into my life. If I play long enough or hard enough will I become good enough to be loved. Just what do I have to do to find the kind of love that will satisfy me for the rest of my life. I am taking about a love strong enough to endure all the good the bad and the ugly that has tainted my life. I need someone who is able to overlook my faults and my failures. Someone who is happy to see me every time and all the time. I want someone who will love me so much that they will go out of their way to prove their love for me. I need someone who is affectionate, passionate and loving to demonstrate just what unconditional love really is. Is there anybody out there that is able to demonstrate a love like this? Am I able to love with this type of love?

Think about your life and see if you have experienced

this type of love and who it is that has given this to you. A mother, a brother or sister, a child or possibly your spouse. Maybe you have yet to experience a love with this type of depth and commitment. Even when we think we love unconditionally there are usually hidden motives in our hearts. One of those conditions is the expectation to experience the same unconditional type of love that we are giving. If the one we are pouring our lives into is not reciprocating this same love, our love will generally wane. Now there are those exceptional people who choose to love regardless of the love being returned. But they are few in number. Generally, a child's love for a parent or the parents love for a child can be unconditional but only because they choose to love regardless of the situation or circumstance. These are my hero's. It is not easy to find someone who will go all out to demonstrate their love for their loved one especially when it is not being returned.

However, there is One who loves with an undying love for each one of us. It does not matter if we love or not, God cannot stop loving us. God is love and chooses to love us. There is nothing we can do to make God love us more and there is nothing we can do to make Him love us less. God's love is perfect. It is Gods desire that we would love Him and love Him with all our heart, soul, mind and strength. But weather we love Him or not, He has chosen to love us. He is our creator and our sustainer. Every breath we take or move we make is by his choosing. His love for us is more than we could ever understand or comprehend. Furthermore, we could never give this type of love without His power and presence in our lives. God's love is the greatest love we will ever experience and if you know and love God you know what I am talking about. Even if God has allowed us to experience great suffering or the greatest abuses His love can set us free from every past hurt or humiliation. God's love is able to set us free from the darkest prison and the most vile circumstance. I hear people say that hate is a strong word, but they are wrong. Love is a strong word. Hate is a learned behavior that comes almost naturally. Love is a choice. We get to choose to love or to hate. Choose love, choose to love God first and foremost and you will see how great life can be.

In the following pages I want to introduce you to God as Yahweh. Yahweh is the personal name for God found throughout the Old Testament. Names carry special significance in who God is and how God wants His people to know and experience Him. It is my prayer that God will be glorified in what I have written and that you will be awed by how far God will go to give you a glimpse of His greatness and power. So, read on and while you are reading remember what God said, "Be still and know that I am God; I will be exalted among the nations, I will be exalted in the earth!" (Psalm 46:10).

YAHWEH IS GODS HOLY NAME

God's name is Yahweh! How many believers have never heard the name of Yahweh or Yahweh is foreign to them? Throughout this book I have replaced LORD with Yahweh. God's holy name. "Oh, give thanks to Yahweh! Call upon His name; make known His deeds among the peoples! Sing to Him sing psalms to Him; talk of all His wondrous works! Glory in His holy name; let the hearts of those rejoice who seek Yahweh! Seek Yahweh and His strength; seek His face evermore!" (1st Chronicles 16:7-11). How can we call upon His holy name if we don't even know His name? How can we glorify His holy name when we do not even know His name? In Exodus 6:2 God revealed Himself to Moses as Yahweh, not LORD or Allah or Jehovah but Yahweh. Due to this fact every nation, kingdom, people, tribe, or tongue should be taught that God's holy name is Yahweh. In writing this book I hope to inspire God's people to begin to teach all people everywhere that God has chosen to reveal Himself in His holy scriptures as Yahweh. As Yahweh God reveals Himself time and time again in the scriptures so that we can know Him in a very intimate and personal way. The greatest promise in all of scripture is Gods promise to never leave us without His presence. Both the Old and the New Testament drive this point home, that God is with us.

Yahweh never stops pursuing us. And He wants us to know Him, love Him and worship Him. It is the only thing that our hearts truly desire. We try to fill our lives with many things and yet none truly satisfy. However, life takes on new meaning when we seek the face of Yahweh.

> "O Yahweh, You have searched me and known me. You know my sitting down and my rising up: You understand my thought afar off. You comprehend my path and my lying down, and are acquainted with all my ways. For there is not a word on my tongue, but behold, O Yahweh, You know it altogether. You have hedged me behind and before, and laid Your hand upon me. Such knowledge is too wonderful for me; it is high. I cannot attain it" (Psalm 139:1-6).

Knowing all this to be true and knowing that Yahweh is the one true God and is deserving of our utmost respect and worship I write this book. My desire is to inspire people to read and study their Bibles because it is in the Word of God that we come to know Him more intimately. It is in the Word of God that we find wisdom, knowledge and understanding. God's Word directs us, teaches us and commands us to live life and live it to the fullest. It is because of my knowledge of the scriptures that I have come to know God as Yahweh and now my goal is to teach His commands to others. "For from the rising of the sun, even to its going down, My name shall be great among the Gentiles; in every place incense shall be offered to My name, and a pure offering; for My name shall be great among the nations." Says Yahweh Sabaoth" (Malachi 1:11). I want to have a part in making the name of Yahweh great by teaching people the name of Yahweh. "And now, O priests, this commandment is for you. If you will not hear, and if you will not take it to heart, to give glory to My name," Says Yahweh Sabaoth, "I will send a curse upon you, and I will curse your blessings. Yes, I have already, because you do not take it to heart" (Malachi 2:1-2). I want to give glory to the name of Yahweh. I have taken the name of Yahweh to heart and I want to help make His name known among the nations.

"His name shall endure forever; His name shall continue as long as the sun, and men shall be blessed in Him; all nations shall call Him blessed" (Psalm 72:17).

"Your name, O Yahweh, endures forever, Your fame, O Yahweh, throughout all generations" (Psalm 135:13).

"So I will make My holy name known in the midst of My people Israel, and I will not let them profane My holy name anymore. Then the nations shall know that I am Yahweh, the Holy One in Israel" (Ezekiel 39:7).

YAHWEH SHAMMAH

Yahweh Shammah[1] - Yahweh is there. No matter where we go, Yahweh is there with us. I love the way King David taught this fact when he wrote Psalm 139. "Where can I go from Your Spirit? Or where can I flee from Your presence? If I ascend into heaven, You are there; if I make my bed in hell, behold, You are there. If I take the wings of the morning, and dwell in the uttermost parts of the sea, even there Your hand shall lead me, and Your right hand shall hold me" (Psalm 139:7-10). No matter where we are, Yahweh is there with us! God is wherever we may be, God is with us. His promise is to never leave us or forsake us and we can stand on this promise and so many others. If you have never experienced God, then it is time. Yahweh, as God, is so awesome and He is love. God is so enthralled with each one of us and wants to reveal Himself in very

---

[1] Charles Brand, Charles Draper, Archie England, *Holman Illustrated Bible Dictionary,* (Holman Bible Publishers, Nashville Tennessee 2003), 1172.

unique ways. Yahweh wants to be involved in every area of our lives and wants us to come to know Him in a way we never thought possible. Yahweh is our creator and we need to seek His face. We will be blessed beyond our wildest dreams if we would but seek Him. If you want to hear the voice of Yahweh, then read the Bible. The Bible is the voice of God. When you read your Bible, God is right there with you. His Spirit is revealing things to you, changing your heart from a hard heart to a heart of love. As we read His Word, God brings times of refreshing and gives us wisdom and knowledge. God's Word makes our faith strong and strengthens our resolve.

When the name of Yahweh is spoken, it should be spoken with the utmost reverence. Yahweh is God, the God who pours out blessings upon us each day regardless of whether we believe in Him or not. God gives us every breath we take and yet so many of us deny His existence. Yahweh wants to enrich our lives and draw us closer to Him so that each day upon waking Yahweh is the first thought in our minds. God wants us to choose to love Him more than anything or anyone. It is what our hearts are truly longing for. The God of the Bible wants us to know and understand Him. This is the greatest reason to learn about God and understand the way He has made Himself known to us through His most holy name, Yahweh.

Just think about how much time and thought parents put into naming their children. A man names his son

David and one day during practice someone calls him a name and it sticks. All his classmates start calling him by this nickname and the boy does not mind due to the attention it brings. However, sometime later his parents hear their son's classmates calling him by this name and they ask him about it. They do not like the nickname because they are proud of the name they have given their son David. And yet they are powerless to take the nickname away and resigned to live with it. Their hearts are crushed but after time it was something they had come to accept. Now most of David's school friends know him by his nickname and when asked about David they do not even know who you are talking about until you use his last name. It was God who put it in the heart of the parents to name their son David.

I only tell you this story to drive this point home. How must God feel that His people do not even know His name? And what is even more absurd is that many Bible teachers, when teaching about the name of our God, teach us the name Jehovah which is not even a real word but a made-up word. When translating God's name Yahweh there was no Y or W in that language, so a J was substituted for the Y and a V for the W. This is how we came to know the erroneous translation of God's name Yahweh to Jehovah. Again, Jehovah is a made-up word. This is what God says to Jeremiah.

"I have heard what the prophets have said who prophecy lies in My name, saying, 'I have dreamed, I have dreamed!' "How long will this be in the heart of the prophets who prophesy lies? Indeed they are prophets of the deceit of their own heart, "who try to make My people forget My name by their dreams which everyone tells his neighbor, as their fathers forgot My name for Baal" (Jeremiah 23:25-27).

We must not forget how God revealed Himself to Abraham, Isaac and Jacob as El Shaddai, the Almighty God and to Moses and the children of Israel as Yahweh. The name Yahweh is used almost seven thousand times in the Old Testament with various other names that reveal intimate details about the awesome God we serve. The following are how God is referred to many times in the scriptures that you may or may not have heard. Do you know that Adonai is translated as "Lord" which means master? El-Shaddai is the Almighty God. El-Elyon is the Most High God. El-Olam is the Everlasting God. Throughout the Old Testament when we read "Lord God," Lord in all capital letters is how we translate the Hebrew name of Yahweh. God is most often translated as Elohim. Elohim is plural for God. I am of the opinion that Elohim represents the Trinity, the Triune God. God the Father, God the Son and God the Holy Spirit. As in

Genesis when God (Elohim) says; "Let Us make man in Our image, according to Our likeness;" (Genesis 1:26a). In the beginning of the creation story, we read, "In the beginning God created the heavens and the earth. The earth was without form, and void; and darkness was on the face of the deep. And the Spirit of God was hovering over the face of the waters. Then God said, "Let there be light"; and there was light" (Genesis 1:1-3). It is not difficult to see God at work in the creation story and the Spirit of God as well. And if you look in the book of John, we find this golden nugget of truth.

> "In the beginning was the Word, and the Word was with God, and the Word was God. He was in the beginning with God. All things were made through Him, and without Him nothing was made that was made. In Him was life, and the life was the light of men. And the light shines in the darkness, and the darkness did not comprehend it" (John 1:1-5).

Not only was Jesus Christ present at the creation of the world but all things were made for Him and by Him. It is awesome to see God the Father, God the Son and God the Holy Spirit all present in the creation story. If you still need convincing read on.

"For by Him all things were created that
are in heaven and that are on the earth,
visible and invisible, whether thrones or
dominions or principalities or powers. All
things were created through Him and
for Him. And He is before all things,
and in Him all things consist. And He
is the head of the body, the church, who
is the beginning, the firstborn from the
dead, that in all things He may have the
preeminence" (Colossians 1:16-18).

In fact, when you take the whole of the scriptures;
God the Father, God the Son and God the Holy Spirit
are at work throughout every story, every chapter and
every portion of the Word of God. Even in certain
books, like the book of Ester where Gods name is not
mentioned. And yet as you read the story you hear and
see and know God is there working in and through the
people; giving encouragement, direction, wisdom and
whatever is needed. And the story has never changed.
God the Father, God the Son and God the Holy Spirit
are still at work in the lives of people today and will
continue to be today, tomorrow and forever! Praise His
holy name, God's name is Yahweh!

"Among the gods there is none like You, O
Yahweh; nor are there any works like Your

works. All nations whom You have made shall come and worship before You, O Yahweh, and shall glorify Your name. For You are great, and do wondrous things; You alone are God. Teach me Your way, O Yahweh; I will walk in Your truth; unite my heart to fear Your name. I will praise You, O Yahweh my God, with all my heart, and I will glorify Your name forevermore. For great is Your mercy toward me, and You have delivered my soul from the depths of Sheol" (Psalm 86:8-13).

YAHWEH ELOHIM

Yahweh Elohim[2] – The LORD God. As I have stated each time we read "God" in the Old Testament it is most often translated "Elohim". The "LORD God" is our translation for Yahweh Elohim. LORD being all in caps. When we read, "the LORD our God" and the "LORD my God" again it is Yahweh our Elohim or Yahweh my Elohim. It can be quite confusing since our English translations use LORD, Lord and lord, which all have a different meaning. LORD all in capital letters is Yahweh the name God used to reveal Himself throughout the Old Testament. How eye opening would it be to know each and every time Yahweh reveals Himself to someone in the scriptures and the exact way Yahweh reveals Himself. God tells Moses "I appeared to Abraham, to Isaac, and to Jacob, as God Almighty, (El-Shaddai) but by My name Yahweh I was not known to them" (Exodus 6:3). God revealed Himself to Abraham, Isaac and Jacob as El-Shaddai which we translate as

---

2 Ibid., 1172

15

"God Almighty", but He reveals Himself to Moses as Yahweh which we translate LORD. When you see Lord with a capital L and small ord this is how we translate Adonai which means master. The word "lord" is like saying sir. How confusing it is since we translate Yahweh as LORD, Adonai as Lord, and lord as sir. Let me give the following in hopes of making it clear.

YAHWEH = LORD, anytime you see LORD in all caps it is Yahweh.

Elohim = God, plural for God, the supreme God.

El = God or strength or mighty and could mean any deity.

Adonai = Lord, which means master, used for God alone.

Adon = lord, which is a term of respect like sir.

Yah = is a shortened form for Yahweh.

"Bow down your ear, O Yahweh, hear me; for I am poor and needy. Preserve my life, for I am holy; You are my Elohim; save Your servant who trusts in You! Be merciful to me, O Adonai, for I cry to You all day long. Make glad the soul of Your servant, for to You, O Adonai, I lift up my soul. For You, Adonai, are good, and ready to forgive, and abundant in mercy to all those who call upon You. Give ear, O

Yahweh, to my prayer; and attend to the voice of my supplications. In the day of my trouble I will call upon You, for You will answer me" (Psalm 86:1-7).

Here is my question. What is a Lord? We do not have Lords in America. England has Lords and even people whose last name is "Lord". And where does the word "Lord" come from? Who decided it would be the word we use for Yahweh in the first place? And why would I want to call the Most High God by the last name of someone else? Lord is an old English word and its literal meaning is "food dispenser". I mean really! Is that who we believe the LORD God, "Yahweh Elohim" really is, a food dispenser? How deplorable and pathetic that we as an English-speaking people could not find a better way to describe the Most High God than as a food dispenser. What is even worse is the fact that Lord is a last name. That's right, if you were to break out your phone book and look under Lord you can very easily find someone in your phone book with the last name of LORD. Does using Lord help in our vain attempt to make God fit our understanding? God has a name that is unlike anyone else's name. Tell me how many people you can find with the name of Yahweh. None, zilch, zero, it's not happening.

When I hear the word God there is only One who fits that name and it is Yahweh the creator and sustainer of everything. Yahweh is also very unique and when you learn God's name as Yahweh, He is the only one that will come to mind when you say or hear the name Yahweh. The Psalmist says, "That they may know that You, whose name alone is Yahweh, are the Most High over all the earth" (Psalm 83:18). It is the same way with the word God, there is only one person who comes to mind when I hear the name God. There is no other God but Yahweh, He is the Most High God ("El-Elyon") and no one or nothing can compare to who God is. It would be so wonderful to find a Bible that would use Yahweh where Yahweh is appropriate or Adonai, Elohim, El-Shaddai, El-Elyon or whatever name is being used by the original writers and then to teach us about the name being used. Please do not get me wrong. I still refer to our LORD as LORD and I am not saying we should get rid of the name we use. I just want people everywhere to know God's name as He has revealed Himself to us throughout the scriptures. "But You O Yahweh, shall endure forever, and the remembrance of Your name to all generations" (Psalm 102:12). I also want people to understand the significance of using God's name in vain. Whatever name we choose, LORD, God, Jehovah or any other name people use for God should be spoken with reverence. I believe Christians are the worst for using God's name as an utterance of surprise, disgust, anger or an exclamation. "OMG" is using God's name in vain. "Good LORD" is using God's name in vain. "Sweet

Jesus" is using God's name in vain. If we are not talking to God or about God when we use God's name, we make His name meaningless. His name means nothing through these profane utterances. Just remember what God says. "You shall not take the name of the Lord your God in vain, for the Lord will not hold him guiltless who takes His name in vain" (Exodus 20:7).

This is just one of many reasons that we should teach God's name to the nations? Everyone everywhere needs to know God's holy name. People don't know that Jehovah is a made-up name. Jehovah is not even a real word, it's a made-up word. How can we praise God's holy name if we do not even know His holy name? Is that how little we care about God's name that we would make up a word to call our God? It is also disrespectful to refer to God as "the man upstairs" or "the big guy" or whatever irreverent name you may choose to show disrespect to God. In truth we all have a name we like to be called. It is how we introduce ourselves to others. If you call us by something different, we are generally offended. When speaking to elders or our superiors we use Mr., Mrs., sir or ma'am or some other term of respect. Why then, would we want to show our God, Yahweh the Most High God, anything less. God's holy name is Yahweh! In my heart and my mind, I know without any doubt that God is real. I have experienced Him in so many ways as I read the scriptures, when I pray and when I praise Him in private. Each day after spending time alone with Yahweh I go off to work with a song in my heart and a skip in my step. I find strength in my time alone with God. I find encouragement, joy, peace, knowledge, wisdom and direction as God guides me through each day. There are times I can feel His presence and there are other times I have to stand in faith believing that He is there. When I find myself feeling lost and all alone, I begin to praise His holy name. And when I begin to praise Him, my heart fills with joy and with an assurance that He is with me. Yahweh is an awesome God and I want to be more than just a son to God I want to be His friend. And as His friend I hold God in high esteem and I want to worship Him in spirit and in truth. How is that possible if I don't know His very personal name? God's name is Yahweh.

YHWH Lord YHWH

Yahweh Nissi

Yahweh Nissi[3] - "Yahweh is my banner" (Exodus 17:15). A banner is used as a rallying point when trouble comes or a call to arms in times of impending danger. We use banners all the time, in ball games or parades or social functions. We use signs to give direction, even as children getting on a bus, there is some type of sign giving direction so they know what bus is theirs. Billboards litter our landscapes and you can hardly get away from a sign pushing this product or this idea or giving direction. A banner however, says run here, our team is here, help can be found right here. When a banner is lifted high there leaves no question or hesitation of where we need to be. As our banner, Yahweh is a Great and Mighty Warrior who goes before and behind giving us protection, helping us in the fight against powers and principalities and the rulers of darkness. Protecting us from trials and troubles including those we get into on our own as well as from the unseen and the unknown.

---

[3] Ibid., 1172

"Therefore behold, I will this once cause them to know, I will cause them to know My hand and My might; and they shall know that My name is Yahweh" (Jeremiah 16:21). God also takes great joy in empowering us to do whatever He has called us to. Yahweh wants to empower us to face the challenges of life and death and every test or trial that may come our way. Moses sought help from Yahweh in the story found in Exodus 17:8-16 when Israel went to battle against the Amalekites. Moses was on top of a hill holding the staff of God over his head and when he would get tired of holding his hands up and drop them the Amalekites would prevail against the Israelites. So, Aaron and Hur sat Moses on a stone and each stood on a side and held his hands up so that Israel defeated Amalek that day. Moses then built an alter and called it Yahweh Nissi, "The-Lord-Is-My-Banner."

God promised Moses and the children of Israel that He would wipe out the enemy. Israel worked together that day to defeat the enemy with the help of their God and this promise is still true today with Yahweh as our Banner. When we are overwhelmed by the circumstances of life, when the battle is out of control or when we cannot seem to find the way out, we have a place where we can run. God does not promise that we will not face problems. However, He has promised to be with us so that we never face any of life's troubles without His presence.

"Through Yahweh's mercies we are not consumed, because His compassions fail not. They are new every morning; Great is Your faithfulness. "Yahweh is my portion," says my soul. "Therefore I hope in Him!" Yahweh is good to those who wait for him, to the soul who seeks Him. It is good that one should hope and wait quietly for the salvation of Yahweh" (Lamentations 3:22-26).

It does not matter that we may fail, what matters is that God's mercies never do. God is with us!

Yahweh is merciful and gracious, slow to anger, and abounding in mercy. He will not always strive with us, nor will He keep His anger forever. He has not dealt with us according to our sins, nor punished us according to our iniquities. For as the heavens are high above the earth, so great is His mercy toward those who fear Him; as far as the east is from the west, so far has He removed our transgressions from us. As a father pities his children, so Yahweh pities those who fear Him. For He knows our frame; He remembers that we are dust" (Psalm 103:8-14).

Yahweh Nissi is a Great and Mighty Warrior who fights for us and protects us and removes even our failures out of the way so we can rest in Him. No more shame or guilt, no more sorrow if we would but choose to believe that God is concerned about us. God goes as far as it takes to be a loving and forgiving God in order that we can have a relationship with Him. In Yahweh we have no fear because we know that He is an awesome God whom none can contend. Yahweh has no equal or anyone that can compare. Yahweh is the Almighty God, (El Shaddai), the most high God, (El-Elyon), the only true God. He is God alone.

> "You are My witnesses," says Yahweh, and my servant whom I have chosen, that you may know and believe Me, and understand that I am He. Before Me there was no God formed, nor shall there be after Me. I, even I, am Yahweh and beside Me there is no savior" (Isaiah 43:10-12).

"I am Yahweh, that is My name; and My glory I will not give to another, nor My praise to carved images" (Isaiah 42:8). God's name is Yahweh!

Yahweh Sabaoth

Yahweh Sabaoth[4] - "Yahweh of Host" who commands legions of mighty angel's and armies of men (1st Samuel 1:3; Jeremiah 11:20; 1st Samuel 17:45). When the soldiers came after Jesus, He made it known to those with Him, "do you think that I cannot now pray to My Father, and He will provide Me with more than twelve legions of angels?" (Matthew 27:53). Not that Jesus needs any help. Remember when they came for Him and at the words Jesus spoke, they all fell down?

> "Jesus therefore, knowing all things that would come upon Him, went forward and said to them, "Whom are you seeking?" They answered Him, "Jesus of Nazareth." Jesus said to them, "I am He," And Judas, who betrayed Him, also stood with them. Now when He said to them, "I am He,"

---

[4] Ibid., 1172

they drew back and fell to the ground"
(John 18:4-6).

Jesus was God and is God and will always be God.
Jesus allowed the soldiers to take Him into custody.
Jesus willing, laid down His life because He knew it was
the only way to save us. In the Psalms we read "For He
shall give His angels charge over you" (Psalm 91:11). It
was an angel that announced the birth of Jesus to the
shepherds and a multitude of heavenly host accompanied
the angel praising God (Luke 2:9&13). We see an angel
come to minister to Him on the Mount of Olives just
before his crucifixion (Luke 22:43), and Moses and
Elijah (Matthew 17:3), who were long since taken from
this world appear at Jesus's transfiguration. There is a
plethora of stories where angels are at his command.
And on numerous occasions we see Jesus speaking out
against demons and they obey His every word without
hesitation. Jesus commands the living, and the dead,
after all we are all His creation as already discussed.

When the king of Syria was making war against
Israel and the servant of the man of God saw the Syrian
army surrounding them, he began to be afraid.

> "And when the servant of the man of
> God arose early and went out, there was
> an army, surrounding the city with horses
> and chariots. And his servant said to him,

"Alas, my master! What shall we do?" So He answered, "Do not fear, for those who are with us are more than those who are with them." And Elisha prayed and said, "Yahweh, I pray, open his eyes that he may see." Then Yahweh opened the eyes of the young man, and he saw. And behold the mountain was full of horses and chariots of fire all around Elisha" (2nd Kings 6:15-17).

What an exciting story to let us know that Yahweh is always the one in command. Each time God reveals His character to us we begin to know more about who Yahweh is and what our great God is like. We get to experience Yahweh in intimate ways that draw us closer to Him.

"Thus says Yahweh: Let not the wise man glory in his wisdom, let not the mighty man glory in his might, nor let the rich man glory in his riches; but let him who glories glory in this, that he understands and knows Me, that I am Yahweh, exercising lovingkindness, justice and righteousness in the earth. For in these I delight, says Yahweh" (Jeremiah 9:23-24).

How great is that? Yahweh says we can know Him

and understand Him. What an incredible thought when you begin to understand that the Most High God wants to be known by us.

> "We know that the Son of God has come and has given us an understanding, that we may know Him who is true: and we are in Him who is true, in His Son Jesus Christ. This is the true God and eternal life. Little children, keep yourselves from idols. Amen" (1ˢᵗ John 5:20-21).

There is another great story that I love to read when Israel and their king was about to be attacked by an insurmountable force. The king set himself to seek Yahweh and proclaimed a fast throughout Judah and all Judah gathered together to seek Yahweh. After praying the Spirit of Yahweh came upon Jahaziel.

> "And he said, "Listen, all you of Judah and you inhabitants of Jerusalem, and you, King Jehoshaphat! Thus says Yahweh to you: Do not be afraid nor dismayed because of this great multitude, for the battle is not yours, but God's" (2ⁿᵈ Chronicles 20:14-15).

Jahaziel went on to instruct the people that they would not even need to fight.

"So they rose early in the morning and went out into the Wilderness of Tekoa; and as they went out, Jehoshaphat stood and said, "Hear me, O Judah and you inhabitants of Jerusalem: Believe in Yahweh your God, and you shall be established; believe His prophets, and you shall prosper." And when he had consulted with the people, he appointed those who should sing to Yahweh, and who should praise the beauty of holiness, as they went out before the army and were saying: "Praise Yahweh, for His mercy endures forever." Now when they began to sing and to praise, Yahweh set ambushes against the people of Ammon, Moab, and Mount Seir, who had come against Judah; and they were defeated. For the people of Ammon and Moab stood up against the inhabitants of Mount Seir to utterly kill and destroy them. And when they had made an end of the inhabitants of Seir, they helped to destroy one another. So when Judah came to a place overlooking the wilderness, they looked toward the multitude; and there were their dead bodies, fallen on the earth. No one had escaped. When Jehoshaphat and his people came to take away their spoil, they found among them an abundance of valuables on the dead bodies, and precious jewelry, which they stripped off for themselves, more than they could carry away; and they were three days gathering the spoil because there was so much. And on the fourth day they assembled in the Valley of Berachah, (Blessing) for there they blessed Yahweh; therefore the name of that place was called The Valley of Berachah (Blessing) until this day. Then they returned every man of Judah and Jerusalem, with Jehoshaphat in front of them, to go back to Jerusalem with joy, for Yahweh had made them rejoice over their enemies. So they came to Jerusalem, with stringed instruments and harps and trumpets, to the house of Yahweh. And the fear of God was on all the kingdoms of those countries when they heard that Yahweh had fought against the enemies of Israel. Then the realm of Jehoshaphat was quiet, for his God gave him rest all around" (2nd Chronicles 20:20-30).

You really need to read the whole story for yourself. It is incredible that Yahweh Sabaoth the Commander of armies is able to defeat any enemy that comes against us if we will but trust Him. How much more does the hand of God move on our behalf when we choose to sing and praise Him in the midst of our adversity? Have you had the chance to sing praise to God when your heart is broken? Or when your world is falling down around you? I have and I can tell you first hand that it does not sound like praise when tears are streaming down your face. It does not sound like praise when your spirit has been broken. It is one thing to have a broken heart, it is quite another to have a broken spirit. Only God can revive a broken spirit. God's name is Yahweh.

YAHWEH JIREH

Yahweh Jireh[5] - "Yahweh will provide" (Genesis 22:14). Have you ever given any thought to just how far God will go to meet our needs? Hagar was sent out to have her baby and found herself lost and alone without any help until Yahweh revealed Himself to her and she called His Name, El Roi "the God who sees me" (Gen. 16:13). How comforting to know "El Roi" the God who sees me. God says, "I love those who love me, and those who seek me diligently will find me" (Proverbs 8:17). Abraham obeys Almighty God, climbs a mountain to offer a sacrifice and at just the right moment when Abraham is about to lose his only son, Yahweh Jireh the One who provides gives Abraham the lesson of a lifetime and a perfect worship experience (Genesis 22:14). Abraham learned quickly how God blesses obedience! How long would it take if we were to list all that God provides for us? Maybe we need to be

---

[5] Ibid., 1172

reminded that every breath we take and every move we make are allowed by God. We exist because of Him.

> "And He has made from one blood every nation of men to dwell on all the face of the earth, and has determined their pre-appointed times and the boundaries of their dwellings, so that they should seek the LORD, in the hope that they might grope for Him and find Him, though He is not far from each one of us" (Acts 17:26-27).

It is truly awesome, the fact that God desires us to seek Him. God wants us to know Him and He is not far from each one of us. Our lives overflow with good things because God wants to pour out on us His blessings. God does not want us to just exist He wants joy to fill our hearts, His peace to overcome our anxiety. God wants to bless us in every sunrise and sunset. We could talk about provisions like food, shelter, hot and cold running water, heat for the cold days and air conditioning for the hot days, clothing, furniture, cars, toys, computers, friends, family, a job and the list goes on and on and on. I do not want to forget about the importance of God's Word that gives us strength to make it through each day, guidance, direction, encouragement, knowledge, wisdom, understanding, correction, spiritual growth and so much more. God gives us people who love us and care for us. To each one is given talents and abilities and a mind filled with awe for an awesome God and a wonderful Savior. The best of all that God gives us is the Spirit of the Most High God dwelling in us. If we choose to seek after God, we will begin to understand just how far God will go to bring us to the knowledge of faith. And I have not even scratched the surface of the many ways Yahweh Jireh continues to provide for us. Also know that just because someone does not believe in God does not negate the fact that God exist! If you will seek Him with all your heart, He will reveal Himself to you and not leave any doubt that He is real and that He loves you.

> "But God demonstrates His own love toward us, in that while we were still sinners, Christ died for us" (Romans 5:8).

I believe it is impossible to fully understand the depth of God's love for us. Just how far would we go to prove our love for someone? How far would we go to prove our love for an unloving, hateful, ungrateful, abusive someone who only uses us for their needs? God went so far as to die for us in the person of Jesus Christ. All sin has been paid for by the death of Jesus on the cross. Every sin ever committed has been paid for by the blood of Jesus. Every sin since the beginning of time, every sin of this present time and every sin until the end of time has been paid for by the blood of Jesus Christ. We have been set free from the penalty of sin if we believe that Jesus died for us.

> "If you confess with your mouth the LORD Jesus and believe in your heart that God has raised Him from the dead, you will be saved. For with the heart one believes unto righteousness, and with the mouth confession is made unto salvation" (Romans 10:9-10).

It is that simple and yet challenging. God wants us to believe and to trust fully in Him. God wants to be involved in every aspect of our lives, and why not, He is anyway. The mystery is just how much more God can do in and through us if we would give ourselves to Him. If you have yet to do this, it is as easy and admitting to God that you have done wrong and are in need of His forgiveness. Then admit to God that You believe Jesus died for your wrong doings (sin) on the cross and ask God to come into your life and change you. Then thank God for saving you.

Now find a church that teaches from the Bible and begin to learn about the plan God has for your life. You might even jump up and down a little and holler and celebrate because now Christ lives in you. Jesus tells us,

"Likewise, I say to you, there is joy in the presence of the angels of God over one sinner who repents" (Like 15:10). Can you picture God's angels being excited and jumping up and down, doing flips and back flips because someone decided to make a decision to follow Jesus Christ? So, get a Bible and open it and begin to read, because if you will read your Bible and pray, you will grow spiritually. Do it every day for the rest of your life. I started this journey back in 1990 and I have read my Bible at least once a year since becoming a Christian. I start in Genesis and then I read through Revelation. When I am done, I start over. It has been the most rewarding discipline ever. God speaks to me in His word no matter what book I may be reading, I receive encouragement, correction, wisdom, understanding, insight, discernment, joy and healing. That is correct, God's Word brings healing. Spiritual, emotional, mental and physical healing. Try it and see if I am not speaking the truth. Yahweh is my provider.

Yahweh Rohi

Yahweh Rohi[6] – "Yahweh is my shepherd" (Psalm 23:1). "Yahweh is my shepherd I shall not want. He makes me to lie down in green pastures; He leads me beside the still waters. He restores my soul; He leads me in the paths of righteousness for His name's sake. Yea, though I walk through the valley of the shadow of death, I will fear no evil; for You are with me; Your rod and Your staff, they comfort me. You prepare a table before me in the presence of my enemies; You anoint my head with oil; my cup runs over. Surely goodness and mercy shall follow me all the days of my life; and I will dwell in the house of Yahweh forever" (Psalm 23:1-6). How often is this Psalm quoted and yet we cannot even begin to fathom the depths God will go to be in a relationship with us. It is the time we spend with God in His word that brings times of refreshing, restoration and great comfort. Still waters run deep and cool and green pastures speak of peace, tranquility and

---

6 Ibid., 1172

37

safety. There is no fear of evil or of the enemy because God is near watching over us. When we believe God, believe in God, believe that He died in the person of Jesus Christ so that we can have an intimate personal relationship with Him; God comes to dwell in us. If we want goodness and mercy to follow us all of our days, we need to grow in that relationship.

If we believe that just because we prayed a prayer or were baptized or went through conformation and now we have gained heaven, we are sadly mistaken. Eternal life comes when we follow hard after God. "You will seek Me and find Me when you search for Me with all your heart" (Jeremiah 29:13). "You shall love Yahweh your God with all your heart, with all your soul, with all your mind, and with all your strength" (Mark 12:30). God wants us to love Him. We all want to be loved. Have you ever had someone love you even with all your faults, flaws and hang ups? Has anyone ever demonstrated an unconditional type of love to you. A love you could be so sure of no matter how far you strayed? Well, that is how God loves us. God knows us better than anyone and still chooses to love us. "God demonstrates His own love toward us, in that while we were still sinners, Christ died for us" (Romans 5:8). God loves us. There is nothing we can do to make God love us more and there is nothing we can do to make God love us less. God loves us! Due to His great love how can we not be moved to love God, to choose to love God? It is by far the greatest choice we will ever make. God wants to be our shepherd and pour out blessings upon us at every turn. God wants us to love Him most, with all that we are. When we choose to love God that deeply and are moved to seek Him daily, our love for others will be very different from the love we have ever demonstrated before. Our love becomes like God's love, perfected through the power of His Holy Spirit. The LORD is my Shepherd; His name is Yahweh.

YAHWEH RAPHA

Yahweh Rapha[7] - "Yahweh heals us" (Exodus 15:26). "If you diligently heed the voice of the LORD your God and do what is right in His sight, give ear to His commandments and keep all His statutes, I will put none of the diseases on you which I have brought on the Egyptians, For I am the LORD who heals you" (Exodus 15:26). As believers we really need to think about what this verse says. Yahweh heals if; we diligently heed His voice and do what is right in His sight. Yahweh heals if; we give ear to His commandments and keep all of His statutes. Now I know we live by the Spirit of the law and not the letter of the law. I know that God gives grace daily and forgiveness comes when we confess our wrong doings. However, how many of our diseases or how many of our emotional, physical, mental and even spiritual ailments are brought on by sin? Think about what this verse is saying. God says He will not put

---

[7] James Strong, LL.D., S.T.D. *The New Strong's Exhaustive Concordance of The Bible,* (Nashville Tennessee, Thomas Nelsons, Inc.), 110

any of the diseases on us that the Egyptians had if we will obey Him so the alternative must also be true. That sin brings sickness. I know that not all sickness is caused by personal sin but I want to be sure to seek God's face anytime sickness comes upon me or my loved ones.

Now remember the most egregious sin is unbelief. As believer's how many times are we plagued by doubts and even unbelief? How many times do we fall into sin and have to cry out to our God to be delivered? Even as believer's sickness and disease are a part of life. However, when I am faced by sickness the first place I go is not to the medicine cabinet but I go to my Yahweh Rapha in prayer. "When I kept silent, my bones grew old through my groaning all the day long. For day and night Your hand was heavy upon me; my vitality was turned into the drought of summer. I acknowledged my sin to You, and my iniquity I have not hidden, I said, "I will confess my transgressions to Yahweh," and You forgave the iniquity of my sin" (Psalm 32:3-5). David learned a powerful lesson from un-confessed sin and notice that David confessed his sin to God and was forgiven. Just how often is it our sin that causes our sickness? "So you shall serve Yahweh your God, and He will bless your bread and your water. And I will take sickness away from the midst of you" (Exodus 22:24). The New Testament is full of stories of people with diverse diseases who are healed through faith and not always the faith of the one who is sick. God wants to bless us and even heal us but

God wants us to live by His strength and power and not our own. "If the Spirit of Him who raised Jesus from the dead dwells in you, He who raised Christ from the dead will also give life to your mortal bodies through His Spirit who dwells in you" (Romans 8:11). I cannot quote this verse enough. It should be a verse every Christian has hidden in their hearts.

If you want a wonderful chapter for confession of sin, read Psalm 51 and even use it as a personal Psalm of confession for your own life. One thing we need to remember is that healing is often conditional and at times God gives ultimate healing by taking us home to be with Him forever. "Draw near to God and He will draw near to you. Cleanse your hands, you sinners; and purify your hearts, you double-minded. Lament and mourn and weep! Let your laughter be turned to mourning and your joy to gloom. Humble yourselves in the sight of the LORD, and He will lift you up" (James 4:7-10). Humility is a lost attribute and one that God honors. It is easy to be proud and arrogant, try being humble. Humility says, "I am not always right". Humility gives mercy even when we do not deserve it. A humble person looks for reasons to help others succeed. Humility is like a healing balm in any relationship. True humility is demonstrated to those who do not deserve it. "Though Yahweh is on high, yet He regards the lowly; but the proud He knows from afar" (Psalm 138:6). God loves humility and regards the humble, listens to the cry of the humble, but resists those who are proud. God wants to help those who can admit their need for help. God loves to help those who know they are powerless to save themselves.

> "For by grace you have been saved through faith, and that not of yourselves; it is the gift of God, not of works, lest anyone should boast. For we are His workmanship, created in Christ Jesus for good works, which God prepared beforehand that we should walk in them" (Ephesians 2:8-10).

By grace through faith we gain access to the heart of God. Faith is the greatest act of obedience we can give God. And His grace is sufficient to meet our most dire need. His grace reaches out to the troubled soul and can sustain us through our most difficult trials. Yahweh Rapha can mend the brokenness of a broken spirit. He is the only one who can. All we have to do is believe in and trust Him. God blesses obedience and obedience brings God's greatest blessings. "But without faith it is impossible to please Him, for he who comes to God must believe that He is, and that He is a rewarder to those who diligently seek Him" (Hebrews 11:6). Yahweh Rapha is the God who heals us.

Jesus Yeshua Yahweh

Yahweh Tsidkenu

Yahweh Tsidkenu[8] - "Yahweh our righteousness".
Righteousness comes by faith! We are made
righteous because of who Jesus is. God died on
the cross in the person of Jesus Christ. Jesus Christ was
God and is God and will always be God. Jesus laid His
glory aside and took on the form of a man and walked
the earth for 33 years and never sinned. Jesus had to be
perfect in order to be the perfect sacrifice. Jesus had to
live in human form and experience all the struggles and
temptations, the test and trials and come through it all
without sin in order to save us. And He did! When we
confess with our mouths the LORD Jesus Christ and
believe in our hearts that God has raised Jesus from the
dead, we are made righteous. Read Romans 10:9-10 and
let it be your prayer and you too will be made righteous.
"For whoever calls upon the name of the LORD shall be
saved" (Romans 10:13). It is that easy. It is the greatest
decision you will ever make. But do not make it lightly

---

[8] Holman Illustrated Bible Dictionary, 1172.

because by making that decision you are telling God that you want to follow Him for the rest of your life. I did it 25 years ago and I have never regretted it.

People say Christianity is a crutch and I say they are lost and afraid. My decision to follow Christ is the hardest attempt at living life ever. I am a former Marine and following Christ is tougher than anything man has ever made me do. And yet it is the greatest journey ever. Now I have the Spirit of the Living God living in me. Christianity is not for the faint of heart. It is a decision that will change your life forever and demand more of you than you ever thought possible. But just for making the decision to follow God, He makes us righteous and holy. We become saints of God in an instant. What a great way to start. It is what Jesus has done that makes us righteous.

> "Behold, the days are coming," says Yahweh, "that I will raise to David a Branch of righteousness; a King shall reign and prosper, and execute judgment and righteousness in the earth. In His days Judah will be saved, and Israel will dwell safely; now this is His name by which He will be called: THE LORD OUR RIGHTEOUSNESS" (Translated - Yahweh Tsidkenu), (Jeremiah 23:5-6).

Jesus shed His blood so that our sins could be forgiven. He made the ultimate sacrifice, His perfect life for our sinful one. Jesus gave everything so that we could stand before a holy God pure and holy. Then He poured out His righteousness on everyone that believes in Him. Jesus made us righteous. "For with the heart one believes unto righteousness, and with the mouth confession is made unto salvation" (Romans 10:10). It's not what we have done that makes us righteous, but what Christ did in our place. It is not about who we are but who He is. Jesus the righteous One. And now that we stand before the Father holy and righteousness Jesus give us this command.

> "As the Father loved Me, I also have loved you; abide in My love. If you keep My commandments, you will abide in My love, just as I have kept My Father's commandments and abide in His love. These things I have spoken to you, that My joy may remain in you, and that your joy may be full. This is my commandment, that you love one another as I have loved you. Greater love has no one than this, than to lay down one's life for his friends. You are My friends if you do whatever I command you" (John 15:9-14).

the high cost of following Jesus? We
ɔve with all that we are and all that we
ɔs it only because He knows we cannot
even hope to love with this type of love without His
help. It will require His power and presence working
in and through us. "He who dwells in the secret place
of the Most High shall abide under the shadow of the
Almighty. I will say of Yahweh, He is my refuge and my
fortress; My God, in Him I will trust" (Psalm 91:1-2).
Have you ever noticed that anything good takes great
discipline and work? If you want a body that is trim
and strong you have to eat right and exercise. If you
want to be good at your job you have to study and work
hard. If you want to play and instrument or be good at
any sport, you have to study, practice and work at it.
Anything good and worthwhile does not come free. You
have to dedicate your life to whatever is your desire. The
question is what are we dedicating our lives to? Since I
want to be all that God wants me to be, I have decided to
dedicate my life to Him. There are times that I stumble
and fall and even fail. However, the end of my story
is already known. I will be with God in heaven for an
eternity because He has made me righteous. Yahweh is
my righteousness!

MERCY AND GRACE

What is the name Yahweh uses for the God of all mercy? Because I have received and continue to receive mercy and I am so very thankful. Mercy is something I do not want to take for granted. I know by reading the Bible that Yahweh is slow to anger and rich in mercy. I know His mercies are new every morning. What about the God of grace? Where would we be without Yahweh's grace? And His wonderful lovingkindness that just fills my heart with awe. Yahweh does not want us to run from His presence but to glory in it. "You will show me the path of life; in Your presence is fullness of joy; at Your right hand are pleasures forevermore" (Psalm 16:11). The more I read about the presence of Yahweh the more I realize it is what my heart yearns for and nothing else can fill that void but Yahweh Himself. "Tremble, O earth, at the presence of Yahweh, at the presence of the God of Jacob, who turned the rock into a pool of water, the flint into a fountain of waters" (Psalm 114:7-8). Tremble at the presence of Yahweh because He is awesome and incredible and more wonderful than we could ever imagine. There is just no God like Yahweh, He is our creator and sustainer who through the power of His Holy Spirit gives life and breath to all things. Make no mistake His presence is the greatest gift we have ever been given. Just one of the many exceedingly great and precious promises given to us is His presence in us. We are also promised eternal life which is a great promise. And we have this abiding joy that sustains us in the most difficult times. Then once we realize the fact that God wants to work in and through us to accomplish His will. God will also allow us to be a vessel of honor using us to take part in reconciling a lost world to Him.

I have barely scratched the surface of the exceedingly great and precious promises and yet without His power and presence everything would be meaningless. We need to realize that Yahweh is real and His greatest desire is for us to allow Him to be involved in every aspect of our lives. The more I grow in the knowledge of Yahweh the more I want to love Him with all my heart and soul and mind and strength. It is the way God wants us to love Him. I want to worship Yahweh in spirit and in truth because that is how He wants and deserves to be worshipped. And I want to know His name! I do not want to know a translation of his name or a made-up word that someone has devised to give God a name. I want to know the name of the God who revealed

Himself to Moses and Gideon and Abraham, Isaac and Jacob. I want to know the name of the God that Elijah and Elisha worshipped. I want to know His holy name. How can I worship His holy name if I don't know His holy name? When I study the scriptures, I find that God's holy name is Yahweh! "Because he has set his love upon Me, therefore I will deliver him; I will exalt him on high, because he has known My name. He shall call upon Me, and I will answer him; I will be with him in trouble; I will deliver him and honor him. With long life I will satisfy him, and show him My salvation" (Psalm 91:14-16). All this to those who have known His name. God's name is Yahweh!

Yahweh Shalom

Yahweh Shalom[9] - "Yahweh is peace". Jesus says, "Peace I leave with you, My peace I give to you; not as the world gives do I give to you. Let not your heart be troubled, neither let it be afraid" (John 14:27). God wants us to have peace in our lives but it is only possible if we learn to trust Him. Once we come to a place of truly trusting God, we can give everything to Him and know that trouble will not come without His knowledge. God wants us to trust Him totally so that fear will have no place in our lives. "These things I have spoken to you, that in Me you may have peace. In the world you will have tribulation; but be of good cheer, I have overcome the world" (John 16:33). Jesus has overcome the world and is seated at the right hand of the throne of God. Jesus is in control even when we feel like the world is falling down around us. Even in the midst of tragedy, trials, harsh circumstances and the

---

[9] Ibid., 1172

most dire state of affairs Jesus wants us to trust Him and in so doing we will have peace.

> "Rejoice in the Lord always, again I will say, rejoice! Let your gentleness be known to all men. The Lord is at hand. Be anxious for nothing, but in everything by prayer and supplication, with thanksgiving, let your request be made known to God; and the peace of God, which surpasses all understanding will guard your hearts and minds through Christ Jesus" (Philippians 4:4-7).

Read these verses a few times and let what is being said really sink in. Have you ever tried to rejoice in the Lord when you are being tested and circumstances have become difficult? When life gets tough, I need to be reminded that the Lord is at hand. God is near to us at all times. If we ever think that God has moved away from us because of whatever crime or offense we may have committed, we need to think again. God has promised to never leave us or forsake us. The Lord is at hand. God says not to be anxious, do not worry. Instead in everything by prayer and supplication with thanksgiving let your request be made known to God. And then the promise follows, the peace of God will guard your hearts and minds through Christ Jesus. The peace of God is the only real peace.

> "Let the peace of God rule in your hearts, to which also you were called in one body; and be thankful. Let the word of Christ dwell in you richly in all wisdom, teaching and admonishing one another in psalms and hymns and spiritual songs, singing with grace in your hearts to the Lord. And whatever you do in word or deed, do all in the name of the Lord Jesus, giving thanks to God the Father through Him" (Colossians 3:17).

Have you noticed that thankfulness seems to go hand in hand with peace? And God does not state whether in good or bad times, just to be thankful. "Rejoice always, pray without ceasing, in everything give thanks; for this is the will of God in Christ Jesus for you" (2nd Thessalonians 5:16-18). Do you want to know what God's will is for your life? You just read it. God wants us to rejoice always and to pray without ceasing and to be thankful. Just in case you feel a little overwhelmed by all this there is something you need to be aware of. None of this is possible without the power of God's Holy Spirit. It takes supernatural power working in and through us for us to live according to God's will. God would not have it any other way. If we will allow God free reign in our lives God will do more than we could ever have imagined. It is His desire that we would seek His face continually. "Now may the God of peace Himself sanctify you completely; and may your whole spirit, soul and body be preserved blameless at the coming of our LORD Jesus Christ. He who calls you is faithful, who also will do it" (1st Thessalonians 5:23-24). Yahweh Shalom is the LORD of peace!

YAHWEH MEKADDESH

Yahweh Mekaddesh[10] - "Yahweh sanctifies me". The word sanctify means to make one holy, to purify. Only God can make us holy. There is nothing we can do except obey Him and allow God to make us clean. When we come to know Jesus Christ as Savior and LORD, we are made righteous. "For with the heart one believes unto righteousness" (Romans 10:10a). That means we are in right standing with God. Our sins have been forgiven but the work of God is just beginning. Sanctification is an ongoing process that moves us into a deeper relationship with God. Sanctification is when we begin learning truth by reading the Bible and lies or untruths that we have believed get replaced by the truth of God's Word. It is when we learn that there is no such thing as a "little white lie", a lie is a lie. Or when God convicts us of something we believe or something we are doing that goes against what is taught in the scriptures. For example, by studying the Bible I learned that "God

---

[10] Ibid., 1172

won't give us more than we can handle" is ___not___ a part of the Bible and it is bad theology. Actually, God allows us to take on more than we can handle and then delivers us from the mess we have made. If God did not allow us to be overwhelmed by life's circumstances, trials or various situations that are out of our control then why would we need Him? Bad things will happen; it is not if, it is when. And when bad things do happen God is there to help us. It is like these verses I have already shared but they are worth sharing again. "Because he has set his love upon Me, therefore I will deliver him; I will set him on high, because he has known My name. He shall call upon Me, and I will answer him; I will be with him in trouble; I will deliver him and honor him" (Psalm 91:14-15). This verse points out that God promises to be with us in times of trouble. It is explicit that there will be times of trouble. However, because we have known God's name "Yahweh", because we know Him intimately, God promises to deliver us, set us on high, honor us, we can call upon God and He will answer us. What great promises!

"But in a great house there are not only vessels of gold and silver, but also of wood and clay, some for honor and some for dishonor. Therefore if anyone cleanses himself from the latter, he will be a vessel for honor, sanctified and useful for the Master, prepared for every good work" (2nd Timothy 2:20-21). We cleanse ourselves when we choose to obey God, confess our sins and turn away from harmful, abusive or shameful habits. We will however, need God to help us in the process. Make no mistake when we are trying to turn from things like pornography, lust, lying, hate, choosing not to forgive others, and a host of other sins we will not be successful in our own power. These cannot be eradicated without the help of God's Holy Spirit. This is the process of sanctification and it will continue for the rest of our lives. The good news is that the more we are delivered from sin the more clearly we will hear God's voice. Sin separates us from God due to guilt, shame and humiliation. When I do something that I know is wrong I do not want to seek God's face due to guilt, shame and humiliation. I feel unworthy to approach a holy God. The truth is that we are unworthy regardless of how good we may believe we are.

"For all have sinned and fall short of the glory of God" (Romans 3:23).

"If we say that we have no sin, we deceive ourselves, and the truth is not in us. If we confess our sins, He is faithful and just to forgive us our sins and to cleanse us from all unrighteousness. If we say that we have not sinned, we make Him a liar, and His Word is not in us" (1st John 1:8-10).

This is the process of sanctification and God wants to be involved. It builds our faith and teaches us to rely upon God's power and not our own. When we confess to God that we were wrong and ask for forgiveness, God cleanses us. We have been sanctified and now we are sensitive to what the Spirit of God wants. Until we sin again and are convicted by the Spirit of God and we respond to Him by confessing our sin once again. After time we find ourselves doing less and less confessing since we are maturing and growing closer to God.

While listening to, Dale Thompson, an evangelist, he said something that has always stuck with me concerning sin. He said "Sin will take you farther than you ever wanted to go. And sin will keep you longer than you ever wanted to stay. And sin will cost you more than you ever wanted to pay". Sadly, I found out just how true this saying is. And it is just not worth it. Sin destroys lives and people. Sin separates us from a holy God. When you read the Old Testament, we learn that the blood of bulls or rams or other animal sacrifices cannot free us from the penalty of sin which is death. Doing good things or trying to be good people cannot free us from the penalty of sin. Only the ultimate sacrifice which was the finished work of Jesus Christ when He willingly gave His life on that old rugged cross. His life for ours. Jesus set us free from the curse of sin and death. Jesus died to set us free.

"And this is the testimony; that God has given us eternal life, and this life is in His Son. He who has the Son has life; he who does not have the Son of God does not have life. These things I have written to you who believe in the name of the Son of God, that you may know that you have eternal life, and that you may continue to believe in the name of the Son of God" (1st John 5:11-13).

Are you on the road to sanctification? If not all you have to do is believe that Jesus died for your sins. Then confess that to God and ask God to come into your heart and save you and He will. Then God will draw you closer and closer to Himself through the process of sanctification. What God wants most is to make us a vessel useful for His use. God's plan is to make us holy so that He can dwell in us. Our hearts become His sanctuary. "Do you not know that you are the temple of God and that the Spirit of God dwells in you?" (1st Corinthians 3:16). The whole process of sanctification is to make our hearts holy because God dwells there. "Behold, I stand at the door and knock. If anyone hears My voice and opens the door, I will come in to him and dine with him, and he with Me" (Revelation 3:20). Jesus promises to make Himself known to those who want to know Him. And I would like to point out that

His commandments are not hard in the keeping. All of God's commands require one thing and if you will choose this one thing you will be able to keep God's commandments. That one thing is love. Choose to love God, choose to love those God has put in your life and choose to love those who are hard to love, your enemies. And where you fall short, ask God to help and He will honor that request. "Now this is the confidence that we have in Him, that if we ask anything according to His will, He hears us. And if we know that He hears us, whatever we ask, we know that we have the petitions that we have asked of Him" 1st John 5:14-15). Once you reach the point of wanting to be used by God and having the desire to choose love in every situation, you will know Yahweh Mekaddesh the LORD who sanctifies you!

Yahweh, He is My Rock

How often do we read in the scriptures God being described as a rock or solid ground? "Bow down Your ear to me, deliver me speedily; be my rock of strength, a fortress of defense to save me." For You are my rock and my fortress; therefore, for Your name's sake, lead me and guide me" (Psalm 31:2-3). One day while praying God gave me this analogy. God is the earth and uses all the forces of gravity to keep us grounded, walking on solid ground without stumbling. God is the path before us and we walk in faith daily with Him as our guide. "Your word is a lamp to my feet and a light to my path" (Psalm 119:105). Gods Holy Spirit is the air we breathe who also empowers us with each breath we take and without Him we could not exist. "For in Him we live, and move and have our being" (Acts 17:28a). Each day we need to breathe in the Holy Spirit and the power He gives us to make it through each day. Jesus Christ is the cool refreshing water we drink the water that our bodies long for. "As the deer pants for the water brooks, so pants my soul for You, O God" (Psalm 42:1). Each day God gives us the choice to come often and drink deeply from the river of life who is Jesus Christ and the air we are breathing is the Spirit of God, who is oxygenating the life-giving blood within us. By choosing to read Gods word on a daily basis we are drinking in life giving water and the air we breathe is allowing our minds to think clearly. As the Word of God becomes our daily bread God is teaching us wonderful things we never knew. God is using His Word to encourage and instruct us. His Word is leading us down the paths He wants us to follow, giving direction when we face tough decisions and giving strength when we face temptation or trials that will cause us to stumble without His loving guiding hand. "Thus says Yahweh who made it, Yahweh who formed it to establish it (Yahweh is His name): 'Call to Me, and I will answer you, and show you great and mighty things, which you do not know'" (Jeremiah 33:2-3). Or we can choose to deny God daily and chase after other things that will not truly refresh or satisfy and walk around in a state of dehydration day after day dying spiritually from the lack of God in our lives.

"But this people has a defiant and rebellious heart; they have revolted and departed. They do not say in their heart, "Let us now fear Yahweh our Elohim, who gives rain, both the former and the latter, in its season. He reserves for us appointed weeks of the harvest." Your iniquities have turned these things away, and your sins have withheld good from you" (Jeremiah 5:23-25).

"For my people are foolish, they have not known Me, they are silly children. And they have no understanding. They are wise to do evil, but to do good they have no knowledge" (Jeremiah 4:22).

We must choose daily to hydrate our spirits through the life-giving Word of God in order to live life to the fullest. "But if the Spirit of Him who raised Jesus from the dead dwells in you, He who raised Christ from the dead will also give life to your mortal bodies through His Spirit who dwells in you" (Romans 8:11).

WHERE THE CHURCH FALLS SHORT

I believe God has me writing this book and I also believe there are others who are also frustrated by the direction of the Church today. I really believe that our worship is hindered by not knowing God at a more intimate level. We need to get back to the basics. How is it possible to worship God the way He wants to be worshipped without knowing His name? The name He wants us to know, the name God used to reveal Himself to Moses and the children of Israel. The Psalmist says, "But You, O Yahweh, shall endure forever, and the remembrance of your name to all generations" (Psalm 102:12). My goal is to remind this generation that God's name is Yahweh and this is the name God used throughout the Old Testament to make Himself known. Again, the Psalmist says, "I will make Your name to be remembered in all generations; therefore the people shall praise You forever and ever" (Psalm 45:17). I have this calling in my heart to make Yahweh's name to be remembered by this generation and those generations to follow. And what has inspired me most is knowing that I am known by God. He knows my name! I love God because He first loved me. God loves me more intimately and more deeply than any love I have ever experienced. Therefore, I want to love God with all that I am and with all that I have. I know I fail daily, but God is worth it. God is worth getting up each day and remembering He has given me another chance to start again. Remember, His mercies are new every morning. So with each new day I am given another chance to follow hard after Him. God, help me to love you more!

In the following pages I would like to share what we do as the Church that takes away from or hinders our worship. These are things I have noticed as someone sitting in the pew fully participating in the songs that are being sung, the prayers that are being offered, the gifts that are being given and the message that is being shared. As a minister I have been on both sides of the pulpit and the following pages are my observations and I believe they are supported by the scriptures. Even though I am quite passionate about these issues that I believe are hurting and hindering our worship, I do not mean to come across condescending or arrogant. As you read these pages, I want to admit that I am a sinner of the worst sort. I say that because I know the truth and still fail daily. I have been set free from so many things and through it all God has matured me and helped me to grow spiritually. I am a saint of God who still struggles with sin. But I know that the hand of my God is upon me and He blesses me daily. I have learned and I am still learning to walk in intimate fellowship with God each day. My struggle is not the same as when I began this journey because of how God has set me free because I continue to believe and walk in obedience. I let God fight my battles and pray for His help in everything I do. I read His word daily and pray. I praise Him in the good times and the hard times. And this is His promise to those who follow Him. "You will keep him in perfect peace whose mind is stayed on You, because he trusts in You. Trust in Yahweh forever, for in YAH, Yahweh, is everlasting strength" (Isaiah 26:3-4). Our God is an awesome God and His name is Yahweh!

CHURCH IS FOR THE CHURCH

How many people are there among us that truly love to go to church? I know I am one of those who love church. I love the singing because it gives me the chance to sing with other like-minded individuals telling God how great He is. It is wonderful! I love giving back to God knowing that it is God who gives me all that I have and has made me all that I am, all that is good that is. I love hearing the Word of God preached. There is no better way to end and start a week. It does not matter how good the music or the preaching is, I know God wants me involved. I know that God will speak to me through the music and the preaching and the times of prayer. God speaks to us so often throughout each day all we have to do is listen. I also know that when we sit under the preaching of the Word of God our faith is increased. The Bible says: "Faith comes by hearing and hearing by the Word of Christ" (Romans 10:17). I also know that when we choose not to be part of a church our faith grows weak and we begin to believe things that are contrary to the Word of God. The point I want to make here is that church is for the saved, church is for the church. It is not for the lost. What is the church saying when we try to tailor services to cater to the lost or those straddling the fence? If we do church and do it in such a way that the church is encouraged to stay the course, taught how to stay the course and even challenged to be the people God has called us to be. Then the lost will want to be a part. Those on the fence will find the faith to cross over and begin to walk in obedience to Gods commands. Just think about what is happening when we are singing praises to God and the whole room is electrified. The people of God are raising their hands, they are singing out and all focus is on the God that we worship. It is absolutely captivating and enthralling. You cannot help but to want to be a part. And if it is something that continues week after week it will draw people in!

If our focus is on the lost, then the church will suffer. God calls pastors to care for the flock. Those who have heard God's voice and responded. When Jesus tells Peter "feed my sheep", Jesus is speaking of His flock. We certainly need to reach out to the lost and teach the lost. But the Bible teaches us that they cannot understand the gospel. "But even if our gospel is veiled, it is veiled to those who are perishing, whose minds the god of this age has blinded, who do not believe, lest the light of the gospel of the glory of Christ, who is the image of God should shine on them" (2nd Corinthians 4:3-4). It further teaches that once they turn to God He removes the veil. "Nevertheless when one turns to the Lord, the veil is taken away" 2nd Corinthians 3:16). Also, "For it is the God who commanded light to shine out of darkness, who has shone in our hearts to give the light of the knowledge of the glory of God in the face of Jesus Christ" (2nd Corinthians 4:6). It is the job of the people of God to reach out to the lost and share Jesus Christ with a lost world. It is an honor that God has given every believer. God has also given each one of us the ability to share our own testimony of what He has done and is doing in our lives. It is the responsibility of every believer to share with the lost around us. And it is while we are sharing and inviting them to church to experience God that they will hear and see God being praised with such passion and enthusiasm that their lives will be challenged. When they hear the Word of God being preached, they will be convicted. It is what the Word of God does. I believe it is impossible to experience a worship service where believers are fully engaged, engrossed and responding to God through, songs of praise, the giving of tithes, prayer and the preaching of God's Word to not be curious and even intrigued. And let us not forget that Jesus said He will build the church. It is not our job to build the church but to preach and teach the Word of God.

When we leave the church building the ministry of every believer begins. Our mission field is in the work place, the school house, where we shop and where we play. It is the job of every believer to reach out to a lost world and share the Gospel of Jesus Christ. It is also the ministry of every believe to encourage, pray for and help one another. Our ministry is doing the one another's. Love one another, pray for one another, encourage one another, bear one another's burden, forgive one another and the list goes on. If you are reading your Bible you know what I am talking about. And this is only the beginning. Jesus gave us a command when He said;

> "All authority has been given to Me in heaven and on earth. "Go therefore and make disciples of all the nations, baptizing them I the name of the Father and of the Son and of the Holy Spirit, teaching them to observe all things that I have commanded you; and lo, I am with you always, even to the end of the age" (Matthew 28:18-20).

Sadly, we have fallen away from the job that God has given us and now look at the world we live in. What a mess. Just look and listen to what is going on in the work place and the school house and even where we shop and play. Listen to the directives of our government and what is being handed down as laws. These United

States are so far away from God that we are living in a day and time of great confusion. Instead of working to change ourselves on the inside we are trying to change who we are on the outside somehow believing this type of change is going to make us happy. The reality is that only God can help us to change for the better. It takes supernatural power to be the people of God and yet so many of us are rejecting Him. It is time for the people of God to step up and be heard. We cannot judge, condone or condemn, but we can share what God is doing in our lives and teach others how God wants to do the same thing in theirs. Start today. Tell people about your relationship with God. Pray for the people God has put in your path and share verses or portions of the scriptures with those around you and then let God do the rest. We need to start talking about our God and how great He is.

> "This will be written for the generation to come, that a people yet to be created may praise Yahweh. For He looked down from the height of His sanctuary; from heaven Yahweh viewed the earth, to hear the groaning of the prisoner, to release those appointed to death, to declare the name of Yahweh in Zion, and His praise in Jerusalem, when the peoples are gathered together, and the kingdoms, to serve Yahweh" (Psalm 102:18-22).

God has given us the opportunity to join Him in reaching the lost. How can we be silent knowing that people around us are suffering and without hope? As believers in Jesus Christ we have the antidote for every problem known to man and we fail daily to offer this hope to those who need Him most. And why is that? Is it because our faith is weak due to our lack of love for the Most High God? Is it because we are more concerned about our comfort and happiness then about the salvation of the lost? "Now all things are of God, who has reconciled us to Himself through Jesus Christ, and has given us the ministry of reconciliation" (2nd Corinthians 5:18).

CONFESSING THE SINS OF OTHERS

In Matthew 18 Jesus is instructing His disciples about the confession of sin. Jesus says: "If your brother sins, go and show him his fault in private; if he listens to you, you have won your brother" (Matthew 18:15). Go to your brother in private. Jesus did not teach them to share someone else's sin as a prayer request which is truly gossip. Jesus said go to your brother in private. It is only when the brother chooses not to listen that Jesus instructs His disciples to get others involved. In the Sermon on the Mount Jesus instructs His disciples again after explaining the high penalty for calling someone "good for nothing" or "fool". Jesus said; "Therefore if you are presenting your offering at the altar, and there you remember that your brother has something against you, leave your offering before the altar and go; first be reconciled to your brother, and then come and present your offering" (Matthew 5:23 & 24). God is teaching us to be reconciled to one another before trying to bring our offerings to His altar. God is that adamant about us being reconciled to one another. God is so concerned about our relationship with each other that God would rather have us in good standing or good fellowship with each other before we come before Him with whatever gift we may have. God wants our hearts to be pure and our hearts are not pure if we are holding a grudge or envy, or plagued by bitterness or full of anger or animosity or jealousy. If we consider ourselves to be a Christian, then we need to realize that God has called us to be ministers of reconciliation.

> "Therefore, if anyone is in Christ, he is a new creation; old things have passed away; behold all things have become new. Now all things are of God, who has reconciled us to Himself through Jesus Christ, and has given us the ministry of reconciliation, that is, that God was in Christ reconciling the world to Himself, not reckoning their trespasses to them, and has committed to us the word of reconciliation." Now then, we are ambassadors for Christ, as though God were pleading through us; we implore you on Christ's behalf, be reconciled to God" (2nd Corinthians 5:17-20).

As ministers of reconciliation we are to work toward reconciling people and not causing them more trouble. How many times have we shared about someone we know that was in the midst of a struggle and we asked someone to pray for this situation? We seldom tell people to pray as the Spirit of God leads. No, we recount their sins instead to make sure everyone knows they are an adulterer cheating on their spouse or they are doing drugs or an alcoholic or stuck in pornography, teenage pregnancy, spousal abuse and on and on. If God chooses not to hold our transgressions against us, why are we trying to keep the sins of others alive by telling others? We are doing God, and these believers a disservice by confessing their sins to one another and it is nothing short of gossip, and gossip is sin. This does not honor God!

How many times do well meaning pastors share prayer request and make sure to mention the sins of the one they are talking about? Again, gossip. I do not care if we are sure we have the facts right or how sure we are about the sin, we should never share the sins of others. There is nowhere in all of scripture that teaches us to confess the sins of our brothers and sisters. It does not matter how someone comes by this information because confession of sin is sacrosanct. This is holy and sacred information that God gives us so that we can pray specifically for an individual. Even more so if someone chooses to trust us with something that is being done to them and asks for prayer or advice, it is not to be repeated.

Again, this is holy ground and if you are a pastor, a layman or another believer this is not information to be passed on to anyone. God says go to them alone! It is only when we are privy to information about someone who is actively involved in harming themselves or others that we should seek guidance on how to proceed. Even then we do not make it gossip, we help them get help by carefully addressing the situation and bringing it to the attention of those who can help.

"He who conceals a transgression seeks love, but he who repeats a matter separates intimate friends" (Proverbs 17:9). Why is it that we wrongly believe sharing degrading and demeaning details about someone else is okay? Is there something that gives us pleasure in humiliating and debasing others? Do we enjoy shaming and embarrassing people? Does it make us feel better about ourselves? "He who goes about as a talebearer reveals secrets, but he who is trustworthy conceals a matter (Proverbs 11:13). It is a terrible thing when someone falls, and the church is so quick to go and tell everyone the news and of course always under the guise of a prayer request. And then pastors wonder why people choose not to confess their sins one to another due to the fact that pastors at times are the worst culprits. In the passage found in James we find the teaching of confession of sins but I believe we get it wrong. True healing comes when we go to the one we sinned against and confess our sins. Confess your sins one to another is when I go to the one I have hurt and admit I was wrong. I hurt them and am admitting my sin and seeking reconciliation. And just how awesome would it be to have the one we hurt to tell us they have already forgiven us because of the teachings of Jesus Christ. And just how righteous would it be to have them pray for us? That is the sign of true forgiveness when it becomes instantaneous. True forgiveness happens when we learn to forgive someone for an offense long before it becomes a stumbling block to us through unforgiveness which causes bitterness, resentment and hate and also invites sickness and disease into our lives. Instead we can choose to be set free by being obedient to God by choosing forgiveness.

"Then Peter came and said to Him, "LORD, how often shall my brother sin against me and I forgive him? Up to seven times?" Jesus said to him, "I do not say to you, up to seven times, but up to seventy times seven" (Matthew 18:22). Jesus is telling Peter to make forgiveness a discipline for life, never stop forgiving. What many of us fail to realize is that forgiveness sets me free. Unforgiveness is a prison of our own making and God will allow us to live in that prison for as long as we choose. When I choose to obey God and forgive those who have hurt me, I am set free. I know how difficult it is to forgive great injustices that were committed against me. I also know how it is to live in a prison of my own making. And how much worse is it when we are finally set free from our past and we are finding our way out when we come face to face with someone who wants to make us live in the past. Once again, we have to deal with the hurt and the pain because people want to remind us of our past and even worse, they want to tell others about our sins. God says "As far as the east is from the west, so far has He removed our transgressions from us" (Psalm 103:12) God chooses to forgive and forget our sins. "For I will forgive their iniquity, and their sin I will remember no more" (Jeremiah 31:34b). So, why is it that the church, our fellow believers, who say they are Christians, want to remind us of our past? Do people realize that they are a tool in Satan's hand doing his dirty work? And how often is it the members of our own family who choose to harbor bitterness and resentment against us.

I can remember countless times as a Chaplain how someone would tell the story of their past and as they do so I am moved with passion and the desire to strike out and punish those who have hurt them. Just like in the movies I begin to hate the villain even though it is their mother or father or spouse or child, or even a stranger or whoever it may be. The fact is, my heart turns against this villain. I can imagine what I would do to this worthless, low down, good for nothing, piece of trash, scoundrel. Wait! How ungodly am I? What I need to remember is that this person they are speaking against is one of God's creations that I am harboring these feelings toward. And what makes me any better than the most egregious sinner? The Bible says "Never pay back evil for evil to anyone" (Romans 12:17a).

> "Let love be without hypocrisy. Abhor what is evil; cling to what is good. Be devoted to one another in brotherly love; give preference to one another in honor; not lagging behind in diligence, fervent in spirit, serving the Lord; rejoicing in hope, persevering in tribulation, devoted to prayer, contributing to the needs of the saints, practicing hospitality" (Romans 12:9-13).

That is one tall order and I know for a fact I fail many times in my Christian walk. God has helped me overcome so many sins but I am still far from perfect. I do know that God will continue to do a good work in me helping me be the servant He has called me to be. We must never forget that we are all sinners! "If we say that we have no sin, we deceive ourselves, and the truth is not in us" (1st John 1:8) "For all have sinned and fall short of the glory of God" (Romans 3:23). Remember it is the words of Christ that give us the best picture of who we are. In Matthew chapters 5-7 what we know as "The Sermon On The Mount." Jesus is surrounded by His disciples and countless others when Jesus tells them "If you then, being evil, know how to give good gifts to your children, how much more will your Father who is in heaven give good things to those who ask Him!" (Matthew 7:11). I do not know how many times I have read that before it hit me right between the eyes. We are evil!

Jesus said it. "If you then, being evil" (Matthew 7:11a). We might not have done certain evils like murder or adultery or whatever sin you want to name as the vilest of sins, you fill in the blank. Or have we? The Bible says if you hate you are a murderer.

> "We know that we have passed from death to life, because we love the brethren. He who does not love his brother abides in death. Whoever hates his brother is a murderer, and you know that no murderer has eternal life abiding in him" (1st John 3:14-15).

Whoever hates someone is a murderer plain and simple. Have you ever held hate in your heart toward someone? Do you have hate toward someone even now? You can ask God to help you to forgive and to help you to love and He will. God loves prayer request like that. Father, help me to love. "He who loves his brother abides in the light, and there is no cause for stumbling in him. But he who hates his brother is in darkness and walks in darkness, and does not know where he is going, because the darkness has blinded his eyes" (1st John 2:10-11).

How many of us are walking in darkness because of unforgiveness? How many of us do not realize that we are spiritually dead due to unforgiveness? How many of us have made the past our god? Out past plagues us daily and it's all we ever think about. Our past consumes our thought life and our focus. We can no longer hear that still small voice of the Holy Spirit within us calling our name. We have turned a deaf ear to God the One who died so that we can live. "If someone says, I love God, and hates his brother, he is a liar; for he who does not love his brother whom he has seen, how can he love God whom he has not seen? And this commandment we have from Him; that he who loves God must love his brother also" (1st John 4:20-21). We cannot say that we love God and walk around with a heart filled with hate. If we are living there, there is only one way to be set free. Confess it to God. Please do not go to someone and tell them you hate them. Instead confess it to God and when you hear God telling you through His word and the circumstances of life and possibly even by the direction of a godly friend or pastor, then go to that person. Confess that you have wronged them and want to work toward reconciliation. When we wrongly believe or are taught by some well-meaning Christian that sometimes we should not seek healing in a relationship because of sexual, mental, emotional or physical abuse I believe we negate the power of God. Let me be clear here. If the person is a sexual deviant still practicing these types of abuses then stay away, far away. But if the person has truly been set free and is living life according to God's Word then they are a believer whose sins have been forgiven. I do not care what the lost world believes. God has the power to set His people free from the vilest of sins. And please remember we may place a certain hierarchy on sins but God does not, God says sin is sin. I am no better than Hitler or Stalin or the man who uses children as a human shield during a time of war. The Bible says we are all evil. We all fall short of the glory of God. We are all sinners in need of a savior!

> "Brethren, if anyone among you wanders from the truth, and someone turns him back, let him know that he who turns a sinner from the error of his way will save a soul from death and cover a multitude of sins" (James 5:19-20).

That is a picture of reconciliation. Someone who leads another to the truth so new life can be given and a multitude of sins covered by the blood of Christ. If every believer is called to be a minister of reconciliation, why do we spend so much time running people down because of their sin? It is not love that fills a person with bitterness and envy, it is hate. Hate is a learned behavior. Instead of choosing to love we are sadly allowed to choose to hate. However, it is not God's desire. God's desire is for us to choose to be obedient to His commands. God commands us to love. You do not fall in love and therefore you cannot fall out of love. We either choose to love or choose not to love and to live in disobedience to God. There is no middle ground! "And above all things have fervent love for one another, for love will cover a multitude of sins" (1st Peter 4:8). God wants love to win out even over our most heinous crimes. God wants our love to win. This type of love is not possible without the power of God working in and through us. It is possible to change a vile sinner to a child of God through this same power. A dog may not be able to change its spots but the power of God can break a man's spirit and renew it again. It is one thing to have a broken heart, but it is quite another to have a broken spirit. Only those who have been there can understand what I am saying. People who have been broken by the power of God stay broken. Life can never be the same because it is lived out in a spirit of brokenness. Broken people look to God with a heart filled with thankfulness. Thankful that God would go that far to bring His child into a personal intimate relationship with the living God. There is no God like our God.

God says our love should be a fervent love. We do not know how to love; we do not even know the true meaning of love. Divorce is rampant inside the church and out. We say we love as long as you act the way I want you to act and do what I want you to do. If not, we move on to the next relationship. The words love, honor and cherish are only a fairy tale. We confuse sex and love thinking sex is the answer and therefore we get caught up in pornography, or having multiple sexual partners, or jumping from one bed to another hoping that someday we will have sex with the right person who will fulfill all our dreams. We turn to drugs to ease the pain of our past, illegal and over the counter. There is no difference. We make work our main goal in life thinking things or power or prestige will fulfill that nagging void in our lives. We tell lies in order to impress or little white lies so we do not have to be truthful with those we care about. A lie is a lie no matter how harmless it may seem. We go about doing good things even good things in the name of God with the false belief that we are being the person God has called us to be. We are consumed with social media even to the point of being dangerous to those around us, i.e. texting or talking on the phone while driving. And then we look down on others because we believe their crimes are more offensive or more vile or more degrading then the ones we commit daily. We tell ourselves, "at least I'm not like so and so". The truth is, in Gods opinion we are no better.

When I think about the word fervent, I think about hot and passionate, something that burns so hot that it cannot be quenched. This is my definition of fervent love. God is love and He loves us and goes to great lengths to express His love towards us. God's love is pure and passionate and white hot and we turn our backs on His love daily. Every day we chase hard after everything that looks and feels and smells and sounds and tastes like love and find ourselves used, abused, unloved and spiritually dead. And every day God pours His love out on us by more blessings than we could ever count. God blesses us with food and clothing and sunshine and rain and people who love us and more blessings than I could ever hope to list here. We exist because God allows it. God even puts stumbling blocks before us to slow us down and make us think or to keep us from harm and yet we continue in the chase. God even allows bad things to happen like pain and suffering, every kind of abuse and sickness and even death to make us stop and turn to Him and be healed. Yet we just curse His holy name and run headlong into one relationship after another spewing hate and discontent, being bitter, jealous, envious and filled with rage. And we look down on others supposing them to be the real criminals not realizing our own self-loathing. We have become so bitter and negative, ignorant of the petty, bickering, backbiting, unloving person we have become. The truth is we are all sinners. God will not judge on a sliding scale. God said if we break even one of His laws, we are guilty. So, we try to dress up our sin so it will not look like sin. We call adultery having an affair. It sounds so much better that way. We tell our little white lies and think we are the better for it. We look to the sins of others so we can feel better about ourselves. We divorce our spouses for whatever reason and then say "God does not expect me to stay in that relationship for life." Yes He does! That is why God says to love with a fervent love. That is why God says to forgive. God does not say love if, or forgive if, God says love with a love that is so pure and so hot that forgiveness becomes instantaneous. We are all in need of The Savior.

Here is love. God put aside His crown and His power and was born a man. God lived life and taught us what love really looked like by allowing those He created to reject the Truth, nail Him to a cross and murder Him. God died on that cross and was buried in a borrowed tomb. On the third day the Spirit of the living God raised Jesus from the dead and now He is seated at the right hand of the throne of God. All authority in heaven and on earth has been given to Him by God the Father. God did this because it was the only way for us to be forgiven for our sins. So now, if you want to talk about something or someone so that you can feel better about everything you have ever done wrong. If you want to point your finger or get angry for somebody doing something wrong or shake your head in disbelief. Talk about the great lengths God went through so that we can be forgiven and experience the greatest love ever given. We do not deserve it and we did nothing to earn it and yet it is there for anyone who can admit their need for a Savior. God died on a cross for us so that we can live in a relationship with Him. Our daily prayer ought to be "God help me to love you with all my heart and with all my soul and with all my mind and with all my strength. Because I know that is the way you want to be loved." But it should not stop there. I want to worship God the way He wants to be worshiped. So, "God help me to worship you in spirit and in truth because I know that is how you want to be worshipped. In the name of Jesus Christ, I pray." And if you want to talk about someone else, talk about what Jesus Christ has done in your life. Talk about what Jesus Christ did on the cross so that you can live life free from your past. Talk about what the Spirit of God is teaching you. That is what God wants us to tell others. That is how we confess our sins to one another by telling others what God has done to set us free.

SINGING SONGS
TO GOD

At times during the praise time when we are singing songs to God more often than not something that we are singing pricks my heart to the core. It is at that time I find myself confessing sin or so overwhelmed by emotion because of who God is that I have to stop and bow before Him in silence gathering my emotions before I can continue. I love singing songs that praise God for who He is. There is nothing like telling God how I feel through music. I do not want to sing songs that tell God what I have done or what I am going to do because I know my heart is prone to wonder and fail God daily. I do not want to sing songs that talk about who I am or where I have been or how broken my heart might be. I want to sing songs that tell of the greatness of God, songs that glorify God for Who He is. I want to enter the presence of God in awe and with heartfelt praise and thankfulness. My question is why the congregation is so often led to sings songs about

God instead of *to* God? If we are to enter His presence with thanksgiving in our hearts why are we singing like we are telling the person next to us about God using, He or Him instead of You? If we are to enter His courts with praise, why am I not singing *to* God instead of about God? We sing "He is God, He is God and His love endures". Why can't we sing, "You are God, You are God and Your love endures?" I cannot understand for the life of me why we sing songs about God instead of to God. I come to church to worship God through every facet, every element and every aspect of worship. I come to worship God! I want to pour out my heart to God and I find it difficult to do when I am led to sing songs about God instead of to God. After all God is present. Isn't He?

> "I will praise you, O Yahweh, with my whole heart; I will tell of all Your marvelous works. I will be glad and rejoice in You; I will sing praise to Your name, O Most High" (Psalm 9:11).

> "Sing praise to Yahweh, you saints of His, and give thanks at the remembrance of His holy name" (Psalm 30:4).

> "Oh, give thanks to Yahweh! Call upon His name; make known His deeds among

the peoples! Sing to Him, sing psalms to Him; talk of all His wonderous works! Glory in His holy name; let the hearts of those rejoice who seek Yahweh! Seek Yahweh and His strength; seek Hs face evermore!" (Psalm 105:1-4).

"Give to Yahweh, O families of the peoples, give to Yahweh glory and strength. Give to Yahweh the glory due His name; bring an offering, and come into His courts. Oh, worship Yahweh in the beauty of holiness! Tremble before Him, all the earth" (Psalm 96:7-9).

What would happen to those among us who have yet to confess Christ were to experience worship where the congregation is so on fire and so caught up in singing praises to God? They hear those around lifting their voices, hands are being raised, and the people are singing with all their hearts to the One True God. The air around them is electrified by a congregation lost in a moment of time with every heart and mind focused on singing praises to an awesome God. Every heart and every mind telling God with one voice that "You are an Awesome God, there is no God like you, there is no God but You." It is what our hearts want to say to the Creator and Sustainer of the universe. I want to sing to

God "You are an awesome God." I want to sing to God of His wonderful attributes. God you are holy, God you are faithful, God you are awesome, God your love is amazing and everlasting, God your mercies endure forever. I want to sing thanking God first and foremost for who He is, but also for what He does.

> "Hallelujah! Praise, O servants of Yahweh, praise the name of Yahweh! Blessed be the name of Yahweh from this time forth and forevermore! From the rising of the sun to its going down Yahweh's name is to be praised" (Psalm 113:1-3).

We are inundated with great songs of praise that all one needs to do is to change the He to You. My heart is broken by songs that are poorly thought out. And please do not make me sing a one liner over and over no matter how good it may be. I will go even further to say that I do not want to worship the cross or lift up the cross or even cling to the cross. I want to lift up the Christ! I want to worship the Christ! I want to cling to Christ! I want to ask every Christian song writer to stop teaching people to worship the cross. If Hezekiah were still alive today, he would grind the cross to powder and throw it in the nearest river. The cross is an implement of torture and the Bible says that "Christ endured the cross despising the shame" (Hebrews 12:2b). The cross did not save us, Jesus' death on the cross saved us. There is nothing great or wonderful or marvelous about the cross but there is everything great and wonderful and marvelous about Jesus Christ, He is an Awesome God and His name is Yahweh!

When I am listening to the radio and whatever song is playing it is like they are telling me about how great God is and I want to sing along, but even then I will change it so that I am singing to God. It is quite another when I enter Gods sanctuary each and every Sunday morning and I am led to sing about God instead of to God. The Bible says; "Therefore I will give thanks to You among the nations, O Yahweh, and I will sing praises to Your name" (Psalm 18:49). "Sing praises to God, sing praises; sing praises to our King, sing praises. For God is the King of all the earth; sing praises with a skillful psalm" (Psalm 47:6-7). "Praise Yahweh: for it is good to sing praises unto our God; for it is pleasant; and praise is becoming" (Psalm 147:1). "O come, let us sing for joy to Yahweh, let us sing joyfully to the rock of our salvation. Let us come before His presence with thanksgiving, let us shout joyfully to Him with psalms. For Yahweh is a great God and a great King above all gods" (Psalm 95:1-3). All of these psalms are directing us to sing praises to our God. And I realize that some songs are to reach the lost that are among us but I believe church is for the church and not for the lost. Church is to strengthen believers, encourage, teach, instruct and even convict believers. If the worship team is doing their job of leading people in true unadulterated worship the lost people among the congregation will sit up and take notice. The lost people among the church will be impacted by what they see and hear to a point of longing to have what we have. And that is the ability to worship God in spirit and in truth.

THE SOUND GUY

Without a doubt my hearing has been damaged from the loud music I listened to when I was younger. I also wonder about those who are in charge of the sound booth. Is their hearing also damaged? There are times the music is too loud to be worshipful. And more often than not the lead singer or the worship team is so loud that no other voice can be heard. I feel like the person is so in love with their voice they feel it is necessary to have their microphone louder than the rest. How many others in the congregation are having a hard time in worship because of how loud it is? It even continues when the pastor gets up to preach and his microphone is too loud. I can remember during the start of a pastor's sermon when a small 6-year-old boy had covered his ears and yelled out asking his parents, "Why is he yelling at us." When in fact the pastor was not yelling but his microphone was so loud that when he did begin to talk, he was too loud. And when he would talk louder for effect I was literally blown away and even angered by how loud he was. This hinders worship! Why is it so necessary to blow the congregation away with the sound turned up so loud? What damage is being done to the hearing of the congregation especially the young ones in our midst? And please do not yell out and ask the congregation to "sing out" when there is no way we could ever hope to be heard over the worship team. It simply is no contest between a worship team wired and amped up for sound and a congregation that are there trying to sing their hearts out just wanting to experience God's presence. I know my own personal preference is to be able to hear the choir/praise team, the music leader and the congregation as well. I have been where this is done and the praise time is truly wonderful.

However, how many first-time visitors will never come back because they were overwhelmed by how loud the service was? There have been times that I have wanted to leave because my ears were actually being hurt by the loudness of the music and still again by the loudness of the pastor and both seemed oblivious to how loud they were. I know that balance can be difficult but it is obtainable. It would be a good idea to make sure the person running the sound is not a rocker who listens to his music so loud that his hearing has been damaged and continues to be damaged through this repetitive method of listening to loud music. I would have told you that my hearing is fine until I had to take a mandatory hearing test and it was after that test that it was revealed to me that I do have some hearing loss. In saying that I know I would not be a good candidate to run the sound anywhere. Again, I know it can be hard to find balance and it is even easy to overlook this problem when the sound is a little loud but more often than not the sound is way over the top. I have even used ear plugs in church, but should I have to?

I was visiting a church for the first time and sure enough when the singing began the praise team was so loud that I wanted to leave. But I had been invited by a friend and did not want to hinder their search for a new church home. Not long into the first song the power went out because of a lightning strike from a thunderstorm. One of the leaders began to blame Satan for an attack on their worship service but he was way off base. God knocked the power out so the congregation could experience worship the way it was meant to be. It was one of the best times I have ever had because everyone was singing and everyone could be heard. It was fantastic. The worship team continued to lead and could be heard and even more than that I could hear those around me singing to God with hearts focused on worship. As the service went on the speaker continued to berate the enemy for losing the sound equipment and proceeded to preach a message but I was so turned off because of his glorifying Satan instead of praising God. I never went back to that church. What is it about leading worship or preaching that we feel the need to blast our congregations? How can a congregation ever hope to compete and be heard over the sound systems we have in our churches today? It is like telling the congregation your voices are not important.

THE CROSS

B efore I begin this chapter, I want to make it perfectly clear that I love the cross. I love songs that are done well like "Man of Sorrows". What a great song and I love getting it stuck in my head. I have the cross as a tie tack and many crosses in my own home and even a tattoo on my arm of the cross. However, I wonder how many of us really realize that the cross in the time of Christ was an instrument of torture and an implement of shame. It was criminals who were sentenced and crucified and made an object of humiliation on a cross. The cross was in essence a shameful, disgraceful and appalling way to die. The cross was the most degrading and painful way of capital punishment at the time of Jesus' crucifixion. In short, the cross was not about jewelry but about the most shameful death one could experience. Now it is everywhere and used as jewelry and a symbol of good fortune and I'm ok and you're ok as long as we have a cross around our neck or on our wall or on our vehicle. The cross has lost its meaning and it is largely because we have taken Christ off of the cross that we have forgotten its significance. It is so much easier at Christmas time since Jesus is in a manager as a harmless, non-threatening little baby.

In America people have more faith in Santa Clause and the Easter Bunny than they do in Jesus and what Jesus did on the cross. People say "baby Jesus wouldn't harm anyone and just expects us to get along and be good people and do good to one another. We need to have tolerance and be accepting of one's beliefs and practices." Here is what Jesus says.

> "Do not think that I come to bring peace on earth. I did not come to bring peace but a sword. For I have come to set a man against his father; a daughter against her mother, and a daughter-in-law against her mother-in-law; and a man's enemies will be those of his own household. He who loves father or mother more than Me is not worthy of Me, and he who loves son or daughter more than Me is not worthy of Me. And he who does not take his cross and follow Me is not worthy of Me. He who finds his life will lose it, and he who loses his life for My sake will find it" (Matthew 10:34-39).

People would much rather see Jesus as the baby in the manger instead of God on the cross! However, it wasn't Santa Clause or the Easter Bunny that was stripped naked, beaten, mocked, slapped, slugged, beard pulled out, a crown of thorns pushed down and beaten into place and nailed to a cross. It wasn't Mohammad, or Confucius, or Buda who was nailed to a cross to die for the sins of the world. They are all dead by the way. It was God in the person of Jesus Christ. Jesus, as God the second person of the Trinity, died a shameful, brutal, horrific death on a cross, an implement of torture. And on the third day through the power of the Holy Spirit of God, Jesus the Christ was raised from the dead and is now seated at the right hand of the Majesty on high. Jesus is alive! And what is even more unbelievable is Jesus who is at the right hand of God as LORD of lords and King of kings, continually makes intercession for us. Even after all Jesus has done for a lost world, He chooses to impact our lives daily.

How many times has God saved us from whatever calamity or self-inflicted pain of the heart or from someone or something unseen and how do we return the love He pours out on us? Do we return that love by spending time with Him through prayer and Bible reading? Do we sing praises to Him or live lives filled with thankfulness and awe? Do we allow the Word of God to challenge, encourage, teach, console, convict and guide us? That is why we have the Word of God. It is another one of God's great mysteries how God uses His Word to do a work in us. God's Word changes us from the inside out. Jesus died on a cross so that we could enjoy a relationship with God. We cannot say we have a relationship with God if we do not have a relationship with the Word of God. Our part is to read the Bible and it needs to be a systematic way of studying. One way is by reading one book at a time or reading through the New Testament and then reading through the Old Testament. The best way is to begin at the beginning and read to the end. When you are done, do it again and again for the rest of your life. You will be blessed if you do. Do you want to have love, joy, peace, patience, kindness, goodness, faithfulness, gentleness and self-control rule your life? Read your Bible every day and do what it says. God blesses obedience!

Otherwise you could continue to wear that cross and believe the "I'm okay, you're ok" lies and continue to try to earn heaven by being a good person and doing good things. You will continue to live a life filled with uncertainty, anxiety and confusion, a life without purpose or direction. You get to choose. God will only be as much a part of our lives as we will allow Him. Sadly, He will allow us to keep Him at an arm's length. God gives us that power. And in the end when our time is over God will not make us spend an eternity with Him in heaven since we did not want anything to do with Him while we lived here on earth. God will allow us to choose an eternity without Him and that is what is known as hell. It is a place without Gods' presence.

I had a hard life growing up and largely due to my own rebelliousness. I never knew my father. I was the second of 5 children that my mother raised with very little help. We never had much for birthdays or Christmas and our clothes were generally hand me downs or used clothes from charities. We never knew we were poor. I always played games with neighbor kids and found ways to stay occupied. Even though I never had much of a childhood I did entertain myself by making parachutes or kites from brown grocery sacks or plastic bags. I also made bow and arrows, sling shots and go carts if I could find 4 wheels. We always played outside and rarely watched TV. I ran away several times and got in with the wrong crowd as a teenager. I lied about my age and started working when I was twelve which limited my time to get into trouble even though I still found ways. I joined the Marines the day after I turned 17 and learned to respect authority in about 10 minutes. I got married shortly after joining the Marines and still had this gnawing feeling something was missing from life. My life was filled with family, alcohol, drugs and anything else my heart desired, and I was miserable.

I left my first wife because she did not fill the large void I had in my life. Two short years later I was married again. I was an arrogant, outspoken, hard headed know it all. I was always looking for ways to find whatever it was that was missing but I did not know what "it" was. After the Marines I began to mechanic for a living since I was good with my hands and had a knack for taking things apart and putting them back together. I worked next to this young man who had a large Bible on his tool box and he would always tell me "The Bible says, the Bible says." I wanted to beat him with his Bible. Instead I asked my wife to get me a Bible that I could read and understand so I could shut this guy up. As I read the Bible, I was sucked into the lives of so many of the Old Testament people and their incredible stories. I found myself relating to them and was mesmerized by their stories. I came to a point in my life that I knew the Bible was written for me. I began to change ever so slowly and I began to grow spiritually, oblivious to the fact that it was the Spirit of God working in me. And for the first time I can remember I could feel the presence of God in my life.

Finally, after about 8 months I was almost through the Bible and I was loaded with questions. It was during this time I knew God was calling me to Himself and the Bible was teaching me more and more about who God is. God used the Bible to soften my heart and make huge changes in what I believed about Him. God was showing me the lies I had believed. Then another nosey family began to invite us to church and we decided to go just to shut them up. I did not want to go since I had been to too many church services and was always bored to death or the preaching was telling me that I could never be good enough. And I knew it! We went anyway and while we were there one of the kids had the bright idea to fill out a visitor's card. If I would have known about it, I would have choked them right there in the church pew. And whoever filled out the card checked the box for a pastoral visit. The next thing I knew a pastor was coming over to visit. During this visit he asked us about our relationship with God and I told him about being baptized at 9 in a Baptist church and then again at 12 in a Mormon church. He asked if I wanted to pray to receive Christ and I knew this was the next step God was moving me toward and said yes. My wife also said she wanted to pray as well. The next thing we knew this pastor baptized us and took us under his wing. We were in his Sunday school class and at his home on Wednesdays for a Bible study. The rest is history. I still have various struggles but God has set me free from so many things. My life has never been the same even though I have been through so much this last 25 years. I am so very thankful for what God has done and continues to do. Our God is awesome.

I have learned and continue to learn to pick up my cross daily. It is how we learn obedience through suffering. Suffering is never easy or fun. As I sit here writing this book, I find myself alone once again. A broken man with a broken spirit. God is the only one who knows the depth of my pain these last five years.

And it is God who sustains me and helps me make it through each day. It is God who keeps a song in my heart and fills me with joy in this most difficult time. It is God who reminds me that it is not about what I want to do but what would God have me to do. God wants me to be in a relationship with Him and therefore I have to make sacrifices in order to do so. The great thing I need to remember is how I am blessed because I make these sacrifices to grow closer to God. I read my Bible and pray in order to grow closer to God. I learn to praise God in the good times and the bad in order to grow closer to Him. I have a church home with other believers who help me stay the course and I also help them. But most of all it is the power and presence of the Spirit of God who keeps me grounded and on the right path. It is impossible to live a godly life without God's presence. Here is what Jesus expects of us.

"When He had called the people to Himself, with His disciples also, He said to them, "Whoever desires to come after Me, let him deny himself, and take up his cross, and follow Me. "For whoever desires to save his life will lose it, but whoever loses his life for My sake and the gospel's will save it. "For what will it profit a man if he gains the whole world, and loses his own soul? "Or what will a man give in exchange for his soul? "For whoever is ashamed of Me and My words in this adulterous and sinful generation, of him the Son of Man also will be ashamed when He comes in the glory of His Father with the holy angels" (Mark 8:34-38).

Try living the way these verses tell us on your own power. How difficult is it to deny ourselves of what we want to have or what we want to do in order to serve others? How difficult is it for us to make time every day to spend time alone with God by reading His word and praying? How difficult is it for us to be thankful in every situation and every circumstance? How can we not when we realize that doing all this is what glorifies God? Striving to be the person God has called us to be glorifies Him. Loving the unlovable, serving the unthankful and even loving our enemies is what God has called us to. It is the cross we bear in order to become like Jesus. I choose to lift up the Christ. Jesus said "And I, if I am lifted up from the earth, will draw all peoples to Myself" (John 12:32). If Jesus is lifted up, He will draw all men, not His cross. I choose to cling to the Christ and not to the old wooden cross. I choose to be "looking unto Jesus, the author and finisher of our faith, who for the joy that was set before Him endured the cross, despising the shame, and has sat down at the right hand of the throne of God" (Hebrews 12:2). When Jesus broke the bread, he said "remember me." And when He poured the wine, he said this is my blood which is shed for you. So, I do not think it is a bad thing to have a cross with Jesus still on the cross, in fact the cross is benign without Jesus. I know without a doubt that Jesus is no longer on the cross. In fact, I know that Jesus is seated at the right hand of the throne of God. But when I see the cross and the image of Christ hanging there on that cross I remember. I remember He chose to suffer. He chose to suffer and die so that I could gain eternity with Him!

CONCLUSION

It breaks my heart to know that God will allow me to say, "God you can come this far and that is it." "I do not want to change in this area of my life." We say this each time we know what God wants from us and choose not to do it. We use excuses like, "I can't," or "I don't have the strength." Or other cop-outs to make excuses why we choose not to give up this habit or a certain bad behavior like unforgiveness or lust or pornography, or being a workaholic and so on. What sin has a hold on you? The truth is that God can set us free if we choose to let Him. It comes a lot easier when living in a relationship with God. That means I am well aware of God's presence; in fact, I practice His presence. When I am driving down the road, God is with me. When I am at work, God is with me. When I am playing at the ball field God is there also. When I wake up in the morning and when I go to bed at night God is there. Read Psalms 139 and know that God is speaking directly to you and your heart will grow three sizes. It is an incredible Psalm.

God knows my thoughts and why I do certain things and why I don't do certain things. God knows me better than I know myself.

Knowing all this puts everything into a different perspective. I have come to realize that God wants to replace every bad habit and every sin I struggle with, with something good. All I have to do is ask God to help me to overcome and ask for forgiveness every time I fail and eventually, I will be set free. And when I experience the freedom that comes from being free, I always question myself for waiting so long to let go and let God help me to change. If I choose, I can continue to struggle with the sin until the day I die and God will allow me that choice. But I cannot continue to use the excuse that "I can't" or "I don't have the strength." What I should say will ring true with each one of us. "I don't want to." Why should I change? It is easier to be satisfied with the person I have become then the person God knows I can be with His help. The truth says "I can do all things through Christ who strengthens me" (Philippians 4:3). The truth says, "He who is in you is greater than he who is in the world" (1st John:4:4). Again, the truth says, "If God be for us who can be against us" (Romans 8:31). I could go on but I think I have made my point.

Here's the challenge. Let's choose to love God with all our hearts, our soul, our mind and our strength. And since we will fail let's pray and ask God to help us in this endeavor. Let's choose to worship God in spirit and in truth and since we will fail let's pray and ask God to help us to worship Him the way He wants to be worshipped. I'm not talking about a halfhearted attempt. I'm am talking about going all out. I'm talking about being head over heels in love, giving it all I've got, leaving it all on the field, no holds barred, loving like there is no tomorrow. Pouring myself out like a drink offering until I have nothing left to give. I am talking about choosing to love God more than anything or anyone and not giving up or backing down or making excuses. If we will do this, I know that God will keep pushing back the darkness and filling us with power through His Holy Spirit, filling us up to the top and overflowing. God will keep calling us deeper and filling our lives with His marvelous light, making us pure and holy and ready for the Masters use. It is what God wants from each one of us. It is the way He loves us. What do we have to lose? Our lives? Is there any greater gift I can give? No! "Greater love has no one than this, than to lay down one's life for his friends" (John 15:13). And I know we will be blessed for an all-out attempt to give God what He wants and deserves. So, let's read our Bibles and pray and learn more about our great God every day. God's name is Yahweh.

"And the Word became flesh and dwelt among us, and we beheld His glory, the glory as of the only begotten of the Father, full of grace and truth. "John bore witness of Him and cried out, saying, "This was He of whom I said, 'He who comes after me is preferred before me, for He was before me.'" And of His fullness we have all received, and grace for grace. For the law was given through Moses, but grace and truth came through Jesus Christ" (John 1:14-17).

Printed in the United States
By Bookmasters